the BIG RETIREMENT RISK

RUNNING OUT OF MONEY BEFORE YOU RUN OUT OF TIME

ERIN BOTSFORD

GREENLEAF
BOOK GROUP PRESS

Erin T. Botsford is the founder of The Botsford Group, a financial services firm located in Atlanta, Georgia, and Frisco, Texas. Certain portions of the book may reflect positions and/or recommendations as of a specific prior date, and may no longer be reflective of current positions and/or recommendations for various reasons, including regulatory changes. No reader should assume that the book serves as the receipt of, or a substitute for, personalized advice from Ms. Botsford or The Botsford Group, or from any other investment professional. Please remember that different types of investments involve varying degrees of risk. Therefore, it should not be assumed that future performance of any specific investment, investment product, or investment strategy (including the investments and/or investment strategies referenced in this book), or any of the book's non-investment-related content, will be profitable, prove successful, or be applicable to any individual's specific situation. Should a reader have any questions regarding the applicability of any portion of the book content to his/her individual situation, the reader is encouraged to consult with the professional advisors of his/her choosing.

Published by Greenleaf Book Group Press
Austin, Texas
www.gbgpress.com

Copyright ©2012 Erin T. Botsford

All rights reserved.

No part of this book may be reproduced, stored in a retrieval system, or transmitted by any means, electronic, mechanical, photocopying, recording, or otherwise, without written permission from the copyright holder.

The term Lifestyle Driven Investing is a trademark registered with the United States Patent and Trademark Office and owned by the author's company, The Botsford Group

Distributed by Greenleaf Book Group LLC

For ordering information or special discounts for bulk purchases, please contact LDI Institute at 2611 Internet Blvd., Suite 110, Frisco, TX 75034 or visit our website at www.thebigretirementrisk.com

Design and composition by Greenleaf Book Group and Bumpy Design
Cover design by Greenleaf Book Group LLC

Cataloging-in-Publication data

Publisher's Cataloging-In-Publication Data
(Prepared by The Donohue Group, Inc.)
Botsford, Erin.
   The big retirement risk : running out of money before you run out of time / Erin Botsford.
   — 1st ed.
     p. : ill., charts ; cm.
   ISBN: 978-1-60832-248-0
   1. Retirement income—Planning. 2. Retirees—Finance, Personal. 3. Retirement—Planning. 4. Saving and investment. I. Title.
HG179 .B68 2012
332.024   2011932968

Part of the Tree Neutral® program, which offsets the number of trees consumed in the production and printing of this book by taking proactive steps, such as planting trees in direct proportion to the number of trees used: www.treeneutral.com

Printed in the United States of America on acid-free paper   TreeNeutral®

11 12 13 14 15 16   10 9 8 7 6 5 4 3 2 1

First Edition

To my husband, Bob, the love of my life.

Few people get to stay married to their best friend for over thirty years so I consider myself to be the luckiest girl on the planet! Thanks for your constant support and unconditional love.

You truly "had me at hello"!

An estimated 47 percent of Americans born between 1948 and 1954 may not be able to afford basic expenses and uninsured health care costs through retirement.
—*Employee Benefit Research Institute, 2010*

CONTENTS

INTRODUCTION

What comes to mind when you think about retirement? Playing golf three days a week? Having a home at the beach? Traveling with your grandchildren? Starting a new business? Building water wells in Africa?

Unfortunately, if you are like many people these days, thinking about retirement might make you want to reach for an antacid—or something stronger. Maybe you can't forget about how the lives of retired friends and family members changed overnight when the markets crashed in September 2008. After years of hard work and careful saving—poof! Like a bad magic trick, their money disappeared before their eyes. And now you are shaking in your boots, worried that the same thing might happen to you.

The truth is, they didn't *have* to lose their ability to enjoy their lifestyle. That's why I'm writing this book. Though I wish I had a magic wand I could wave and restore the savings and chosen lifestyles of those who lost so much, that's not reality. What I *can* do is help you not only avoid similar calamity but also become wiser and learn to protect and sustain your lifestyle throughout retirement.

What has become incredibly clear to me in the last decade, particularly since September 2008, is that people's confidence in just about everything has been shattered. As a member myself of the baby boom generation, I can relate to every bit of shakiness that comes with a lack of certainty about the future. I think you will agree that, more than anything, we all want to be assured that we will not run out of money before we take our last breath. Almost equally important, we would like to know that we will not become a burden to our children or to society. As retirees, or pre-retirees getting ready to exit the workplace, we can't help but ask ourselves, "Do I have enough money? Will it last my lifetime? What about my spouse? My children? Is there a chance I will be forced to go back to work? Will Social Security be there when I am eligible to receive it? What about Medicare? Will my pension survive and continue to pay me?" These are all incredibly important questions and ones I am sure you have asked yourself. Though I may not be able to answer these questions for you individually, I feel certain I can help you answer some of them for yourself.

I had one specific goal in mind when I decided to write this book: to restore the lost confidence among the retiree and pre-retiree crowd. It's no fun working for forty or fifty years, becoming an expert in your field, and then having no faith in your ability to sustain your lifestyle throughout your retirement. I want to show you that if you rethink how you make your investment decisions and adopt a new philosophy about money you can regain some of your lost confidence. I believe you can have the retirement you have always dreamed about. But I also believe many people will not be able to live that dream if they don't make some major shifts in the way they think about their money and how they manage their investments.

Unfortunately, many people are still investing the same way they have for the past thirty or forty years, not realizing how significantly the world of investing has changed. The old methods clearly won't work anymore, but many people have no idea what will work. The overwhelming majority of retirement planning and investing is still done with the premise that the stock and/ or bond markets will always go up over the long term. But the two most important questions to ask are these: is that always true, and how long is long term? History shows us multiple decades in which this premise has not been the case. If someone is unfortunate enough to retire when the market goes flat or during a protracted down market, he or she faces the real risk of running out of money.

With this book I hope to show you an entirely new way to think about money, investing, and retirement planning. I am going to shatter the myths of Wall Street, which serve their purposes but could be disastrous to you and your retirement well-being. I will expose the failures inherent in traditional methods of retirement planning, and I will give you a new way to think about money and investing, a concept I have created over the last two decades called Lifestyle Driven Investing. You will quickly see how easy it is and how much it can take the guesswork out of investing for retirement.

In the following chapters, I explain why traditional methods of retirement planning, such as taking systematic withdrawals from balanced portfolios, may not work for you. My objective is to teach you how to create your "Preferred Lifestyle." Your Preferred Lifestyle is the ability to do what you want, when you want and with whom you want, and to sustain it through good economic times and bad. You will learn the difference between "Lifestyle," "Hybrid," and "Non-Lifestyle" investments as part of building a purposeful and strategic investment portfolio so you never have to wonder why you own the investments you own.

In the first chapter of this book, you will read my story—the good, the bad, and the ugly circumstances that were dealt to me early in life. Those circumstances gave me the incentive to learn everything I could about money and investing so I could help prevent others from trusting the wrong people and making the same mistakes I made. You will see that I have spent the better part of my life learning what works and what doesn't work. Keep in mind I have often had to go against the grain in order to maintain what I refer to as an agnostic point of view when it comes to investment product recommendations. When I use the term "agnostic," I am not referring to my religious beliefs but to taking a totally unbiased view of product solutions for the clients who come into my office.

In order to retire, you are going to have to put your money somewhere. Your choice may be to hide it under your mattress, to bury it in a tin can in your backyard, or, if you are a little more mainstream, to put it in financial instruments such as bank accounts, stocks, bonds, and real estate. I understand that changing the way you think about money and investing takes time. When you have finished reading this book, I hope you will think differently. I hope you will feel empowered to challenge the status quo. I want you to be able to ask your financial advisor why he thinks his method of investing is still viable and how he thinks his advice will allow you to retire with the confidence that you will not run out of money. I want you to know why you own what you own, and I don't want you to blindly take anyone's advice, ever again. I believe you will love the world of Lifestyle Driven Investing, which has been designed so you won't run out of money before you run out of time.

CHAPTER 1

WHAT DRIVES YOUR DECISIONS?

If you are like me, your life and the way you make decisions about everything, including money, is a result of the many experiences you have had. Some of those experiences have been good and some have been bad, but clearly—and often unconsciously—they have had an impact on the way you look at the world and how you formulate your decisions. When it comes to making decisions about your money, you can't help but be guided by certain things: what you have read or heard; lessons you learned personally or by watching others; experiences from early in your childhood; and beliefs you were taught by your parents and others as you grew up. In my case, in addition to the more traditional ways one develops beliefs about money, several personal tragedies in my early years shaped my goals, my career, and the way I counsel clients on managing their money. They are the impetus for almost everything I do, including writing this book.

The first time tragedy struck, I was eleven years old. I grew up in a comfortable, middle-class home in the Midwest with loving parents. My father was a highly educated man, a psychology professor in the Chicago area, but he had always dreamed of opening a clinic for early childhood education in Southern California. In his efforts to realize his dream and also create a better life for our family, he took a leap of faith. He quit his job and borrowed against his teacher's pension to move our family to the West Coast. He took a job selling cars to earn money while he waited for his teaching certificate to arrive. It never did. Six months after we moved to California, on Valentine's Day, my father collapsed. He died of a massive heart attack in front of my mother, my siblings, and me. He was fifty years old.

In an instant, our lives changed forever. My father left our family a $10,000 life insurance policy—that was it. He never imagined that he wouldn't be there to realize his dream or provide for the family he cherished. Since he had borrowed against his teacher's pension, there was no benefit available for our family. We went from being middle class to broke overnight.

From that day forward, everyone in our family had to work. My mother needed all of us to pull our weight financially just to keep the lights on. I got my first job before I turned twelve, and, from a young age, I learned the power of a strong work ethic.

We were barely scraping by when tragedy struck again. I was sixteen years old, driving to my first "real" job at McDonald's, when I was involved in a terrible accident with a motorcyclist. The driver of the motorcycle was killed, and I was charged with involuntary manslaughter. My mother and I met with an attorney and were honest about our family's financial situation.

After hearing our story, he spoke to my mother as if I were not even there. "Mrs. McGowan," he said, "this is purely a matter of economics. If your daughter will plead guilty, I will be happy to enter the plea at no charge to you. Your daughter will get the appropriate sentence prescribed by the State of California. But if she wants to defend herself, it will cost you a lot of money."

Since we had no money, my mother realized in an instant our choices were limited. She thanked the attorney and agreed with his advice that I had no option other than to plead guilty. I was horrified. I begged and pleaded with my mother. That's when she looked at me and said the ten words I will never forget: "Honey, we have no money; therefore, we have no choice." That was the day I learned money buys you choices. Fortunately, the case wasn't closed. My older brother, Tim, had just begun his real estate career; he suggested we take out a second mortgage on our home to pay for my defense. With the money from the mortgage, our attorney was able to bring in expert witnesses who proved that the motorcyclist was driving well over the speed limit, and that he had hit me, not the other way around. The judge dropped all the charges. At the end of the court proceeding, he said: "Take this little girl home. She's been through enough."

I wish the story ended there, but it didn't. Shortly after the criminal proceeding, the family of the young motorcyclist sued my mother and me for a substantial sum of money. My mother was terrified that we would lose the only asset she possessed, our family home. She lived with this fear for many years until the case was finally settled at the eleventh hour by our auto insurance company, which came to my defense.

Money can't buy you happiness, but it can buy you choices.

After losing my father, suffering severe financial difficulties, and enduring both a criminal proceeding and a civil lawsuit, I realized the importance of these lessons about money. Following the accident, I became a workaholic, maintaining several jobs so I could earn enough to pay back my mother and put myself through college. I realized the only way for me to get out of poverty was to work hard and get a good education.

Through my diligent saving and a fortuitous winning appearance on *Wheel of Fortune* (ironically, I won by solving the puzzle "Down in the dumps"), I accumulated a nest egg of about $22,000, which was no small sum in 1979. Shortly before I got married, I invested $3,000 to buy a townhouse in San Diego County with a friend. This investment worked out well. Soon after we married, however, my husband, Bob, and I entrusted the balance of our savings to a stockbroker, assuming we were being smart by investing our "wealth" for future growth. The stockbroker divided our money among four different investments, none of which was appropriate for us. All four investments went belly-up in a very short period of time, and we lost every cent we had entrusted to him.

I was devastated. While it may not have been much money to our broker, it was everything to us, and it represented years and years of hard work and sacrifice. I felt stupid, betrayed, and embarrassed. From that day forward, I made it my personal mission to learn everything I could about money and investing. I was determined never to let what happened to us happen to anyone I cared about.

I share my story not to garner pity but rather to explain the impetus behind my philosophy of money. I learned from an early age what poor financial planning—or, worse yet, *no* financial planning—can do to a family. The lessons of poverty have not vanished from my memory. I know from firsthand experience that without money I could have landed in jail. With no ability to prove my innocence, my very freedom could have been taken away from me. Accidents can happen in an instant. Without good planning, an accident that results in a civil lawsuit can threaten to take away everything you have worked so hard to achieve.

Life happens. Accidents happen. Stock markets happen. Markets go up. Markets go down. I've experienced all of this myself, and I have dedicated the better part of my life to helping people find their way through the numerous minefields that threaten to take away their ability to enjoy the fruits of their labor.

By sharing my story and the lessons I have learned about money and investing, I hope to help you wade through the common pitfalls and provide you with the tools and insights to circumvent them. At the same time, I'll share with you what I believe are the best strategies to manage your wealth in retirement so you can live the lifestyle you've always envisioned—regardless of what the markets do.

Keep in mind, my strategies for money management are far from conventional. Because of all I have seen in both my personal and my professional life, I am somewhat cynical when it comes to traditional money management and investment strategies. However, I have not created my strategies in a vacuum. I have studied and followed economists and experts whom I believe are far more learned than I am. What many of them have prescribed in books, I put into practice. I am looking forward to sharing my decades of knowledge with you.

CHAPTER 2

THE FOUR MYTHS OF WALL STREET

O nce I had a client call me with a question that took me by surprise. The client, who was worth about $22 million, asked me, "Erin, do you think I have enough money to buy a Corvette?" I had to laugh. I answered: "Yes, you can afford to buy a Corvette. In fact, you can probably afford to put a down payment on a Corvette dealership!" That question made me realize that even people whom many would consider wealthy are often not confident about how much money it takes to sustain their lifestyles. Though I knew this client had enough money to buy any car he wanted, he wasn't so sure. Nor did he feel enough certainty in his overall financial future to make that purchase without double-checking with me.

Clearly, worrying about money has become a national pastime. These days, finance-related anxiety tends to occupy the minds of almost everyone. Rich or poor, few seem to have much confidence in their financial future. For those who are not wealthy, the fear of running out of money is so pervasive it's verging on epidemic. For those who are considered wealthy, this is sometimes only the beginning of their worries. A recent *USA Today* poll showed that Americans between the ages of forty-four and seventy-five are more afraid of running out of money than of dying. A whopping 61 percent of people in this age group identify being financially insolvent as their foremost fear, whereas only 39 percent list fear of death!

While this may seem counterintuitive, wealthy people sometimes have greater fears about money than other people do. Maybe this is because wealthy people have so many things they can choose to worry about! Some of them worry about the economy and what it might do to their business. Others have made it to the pinnacle of their corporate careers and worry about losing their position, status, and high income due to being fired or laid off. More recently, people who once assumed they had enough money now worry they could lose it all in the next Bernie Madoff–type scandal.

Then there is the risk of someone getting injured in an accident while you or one of your children is driving a car, or of someone getting hurt while visiting your property. What happens if you find yourself in a lawsuit as a result? Wealthy people with multiple rental properties, ranches, boats, jet skis, horses, and other "toys" are particularly vulnerable to these additional risks. They may wonder, "Which of my assets could be taken away from me if I got sued?" If they haven't asked themselves that question, they certainly should!

What happens if you get a divorce after twenty-five years of marriage and must suddenly fend for yourself? What about the issue of health care? What if you or your spouse becomes sick or disabled? What about the costs of nursing homes or home health care if one of you were to get a debilitating disease? Or what if it falls to you to care for aging, elderly, or sick parents? This is becoming increasingly common as life spans lengthen, and if your parents are in their eighties or nineties, chances are they have already used big portions of their nest eggs too.

While many people may have asked themselves these difficult questions in the quiet recesses of their minds, the answers were probably so scary they didn't dare verbalize them. Hence, they rarely do anything to address the issues—until it's too late.

Of course we all want to hope and believe that bad things will never happen to us. We want to believe that if we simply play by the rules and invest wisely we will have enough money to eventually live happily ever after. Unfortunately, life doesn't always work out that way.

I'm not saying that happily ever after doesn't exist. I believe you can achieve the retirement you have always dreamed of, which includes pursuing your favorite hobbies, spending time with your family, and enjoying the fruits of your labor throughout your golden years. However, it is my belief that you will be unable to secure these dreams by following traditional financial planning advice. Why? Because today's economy is radically different from the economy of forty or fifty years ago, the era in which the models currently used by many financial planners were built.

A lot has happened in the past half century. Though credit cards existed in the 1950s, they didn't become a part of everyday life until the 1980s. Online trading started a decade later, giving retail investors access to information previously available only to professionals and thereby revolutionizing the way millions of people invest. Other radical changes, such as the fall of the Soviet

Union and international communism, the creation of the European Union, the collapse of the Japanese "miracle" economy, the rise of new emerging market giants like China and India, and the fallout from the housing crisis of 2008 have had profound impacts on our nation's financial security. The same rules simply no longer apply.

Yet, while the world has been changing at warp speed, many Americans and their advisors seem to be stuck in the past. Enraptured by the go-go '90s, countless investors still believe that the stock market losses of the past decade were a fluke. They continue to hope for a return to the "good old days," not understanding that those days of consistently high returns may have been the fluke.

In this chapter, I am going to share with you what I call "The Four Myths of Wall Street." If people continue to buy into these myths, I believe they will be facing the biggest risk of all: running out of money before they run out of time. But you don't have to be among those ranks.

Life changes, market conditions change, economies change—therefore, *you* must change. Let's examine the most common money myths so you can ditch them and move forward with confidence.

MYTH #1: IN THE LONG TERM, THE STOCK MARKET ALWAYS GOES UP

The myth that the stock market always goes up has been around a long while. From the time you started your first 401(k), you've likely been told that if you invested in the stock market regularly and left your investments alone, over time you would realize an average return of at least 10 percent. That sounded pretty good and relatively easy, didn't it? Sure, some years the market would be up more than 10 percent, and some years the market could actually be down, but over the course of your working life, your returns would all average to that magic number of 10 percent per year. How wonderfully predictable!

There are so many problems with this thinking that it's hard to know where to start. I suppose we should begin by asking, "How long is long term?" Those who claim that stocks *always* return an average of 10 percent usually base their claim on studies of stock returns dating back to the 1920s or even the 1870s. But even if we concede that stock returns from the preindustrial 1870s are relevant to today—which is a stretch, to say the least—you're still looking at only fourteen decades' worth of data. And in many of those decades, returns were negative. We just lived through one of them, in fact.

In a few cases, we have had bear markets that lasted for more than 20 years—and this doesn't include additional value lost to inflation. The reality is that there have been a number of twenty-year periods when the stock market has not produced anything close to the long-term average. Some years it was up 20 percent and other years it was down 30 percent. The graph in Figure 2.1 illustrates the volatile nature of the Dow Jones over the last 113 years. More important to this discussion, it also shows multiple periods of eighteen, twenty-five, and seventeen years where the markets were down or flat. The two questions to ask yourself as you review this chart are "Does the way I am investing for retirement assume that the financial markets will go up?" And "If the markets stay flat or go down for a decade or more, will my current investment strategy allow me to sustain my desired lifestyle?"

DOW JONES HISTORICAL TRENDS

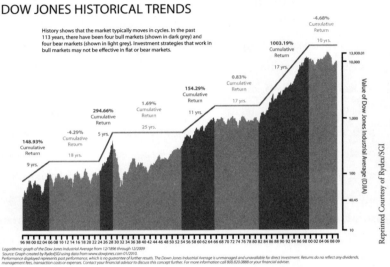

Figure 2.1: Dow Jones Historical Trends

In my opinion, because of the current economic environment in which we live, using some of the traditional investment strategies that many people are using today could be a recipe for disaster. Just because something worked in a defined period sometime in the past does not necessarily mean it will work in the future. Basing your retirement investment strategy on the myth that stocks always go up over the "long term" seems a little like shooting craps to me. You may not have long enough to wait for the long-term returns that Wall Street promises.

MYTH #2: DIVERSIFICATION AND ASSET ALLOCATION ARE THE KEYS TO RETIREMENT SUCCESS

Many financial planners will acknowledge that the markets are fickle and stock portfolios can sometimes be hit hard during bear markets. The key to retirement success, they claim, is to diversify. Their recommended strategy is to allocate your investments among small-cap, mid-cap, and large-cap holdings and across a range of industry sectors. In addition, they use some formula to add fixed income investments, such as bonds and cash holdings, to your portfolio. They top it all off with darlings like international and emerging market portfolios, claiming they've got a recipe for success. This approach, they say, will protect you from the ups and downs of the economy and ensure that you can keep your nest egg throughout retirement. Really? I guess they weren't around in 2008 when everything decreased in value at the same time.

The important question in my mind is whether your nest egg will generate enough *income* for you to maintain the lifestyle you want. The problem with traditional diversification and asset allocation is that there is a fundamental disconnect between the investments—stocks, bonds, real estate, etc.—and the *cash flow* requirements they are supposed to fund. Specifically, how does one receive income from their portfolio?

Retirement planning is not purely a matter of whether you have a big enough number on your balance sheet. I have seen many people with very large numbers on their balance sheets run out of money before running out of time. The key is to convert a portion of that balance sheet number into appropriate investment vehicles that will generate sufficient income for you to live on in good times and bad. Traditional asset allocation models using systematic withdrawals usually work well in markets that are going up, but they can be devastating for retirees in markets that are going sideways or down.

The problem with traditional diversification and asset allocation is that there is a fundamental disconnect between the investments— stocks, bonds, real estate, etc.—and the *cash flow* requirements they are supposed to fund.

MYTH #3: INVESTING THROUGH A MAJOR FINANCIAL SERVICES FIRM GIVES YOU MORE OPTIONS

Let's assume you already recognize the perils of traditional financial planning and you want to branch out beyond stocks, bonds, mutual funds, and exchange-traded funds (ETFs) to other types of investments. You may think entrusting your wealth to one of the large brokerage houses or investment banking firms is the way to go. After all, if they're among the biggest players on Wall Street, they must offer the best options for managing your money, right? Think again.

The truth is they offer the best options for their own money— their own proprietary accounts—which became obvious in 2008 when some of the investment banks actually bet against the mortgage securities they were selling their clients.

Because the major investment firms handle the assets of millions of individual investors, they simply cannot customize their offerings to each individual's needs. Instead, they often appeal to the lowest common denominator, so they generally offer a lot of "vanilla" investment products to their retail clients. It makes sense. The primary objective of the major firms is to make money for the house and to limit their risk. A large firm cannot take the risk that its tens of thousands of registered representatives will be able to adequately explain the features, benefits, and, more importantly, the risks of the more sophisticated strategies. Since this would create a huge liability to the firm, they tend to keep their retail offerings very simple.

It should come as no surprise then that the better vehicles for protecting your lifestyle and achieving a predictable income are often found outside of Wall Street. If this is what you are looking for, your best advice may come from an experienced independent planner who is not as handcuffed by the limitations imposed by the larger firms.

MYTH #4: YOUR NET WORTH DETERMINES YOUR LIFESTYLE IN RETIREMENT

Do you know your "magic number"? Many financial advisors will tell you that you need to amass a certain amount of wealth prior to retirement, a magic number that will let you sail smoothly through your golden years in style and comfort. How ridiculous!

Let me give you an example of the folly of focusing solely on net worth or a magic number. Imagine that you have in your possession a famous Renoir painting you inherited from a rich aunt. Valued at $10 million, it is the single largest asset you possess, and you proudly have it hanging in the living room of your home. If you create a balance sheet, you have an amazing net worth based on that one asset alone. But the problem is, can you eat off of it? Can you sell off little pieces of your painting to pay your monthly bills? The answer, of course, is no. Hence, in many cases, your net worth has no relevance to your lifestyle if it isn't in a form that can quickly be converted to cash to provide for your everyday living expenses. Though it may be a marvel to admire, the Renoir is not an income-producing asset and thus cannot support your lifestyle—unless you can get people to pay you to come into your home to view this remarkable painting. *Then* you will have created some cash flow!

> Your net worth has no relevance to your lifestyle if it isn't in a form that can quickly be converted to cash to provide for your everyday living expenses.

Another reason the magic number isn't so magical is because, in the traditional investment world, there are typically no guarantees once you reach it. Tens of thousands, if not hundreds of thousands, of Americans have been forced to postpone their retirement, and thousands more who were already retired have been forced to reenter the job market after watching their magic number vanish into thin air. Calculating your retirement goal is not the problem. That's the easy part. The problem is determining what to do with the money once you reach your goal so it will sustain you throughout retirement.

In an article for the Associated Press, "Retirement savings goal is no magic number," finance writer Dave Carpenter interviewed a fifty-one-year-old woman who began calculating her magic number in her twenties. With a six-figure income as an IT consultant and a history of aggressive saving and frugal living, she seemed to be on target for reaching her goal. But the market crash of 2008 wiped out 40 percent of her savings; on top of that, she faced a divorce and a layoff. She's had to stop obsessing about her magic number because it is no longer a realistic possibility.

The question I'd ask this woman is, "What are you going to do with the money you still have?" Ask yourself the same question. Should you invest your money in the stock market, bonds, real estate, or some other investment vehicle? What if you are two years and $20,000 away from achieving your magic number and the markets take a nosedive? What if you already achieved your magic number and are enjoying the retirement of your dreams when a market crash causes you to lose 40 percent of your money, like the woman Dave Carpenter interviewed? If you are relying on portfolio withdrawals and suddenly the market tanks, you have a big problem. Can you downsize your expenses without diminishing your lifestyle? I doubt it. Your vision for the future then becomes an impossible dream.

GAMBLING WITH YOUR FUTURE

Unfortunately, the financial advice that has been preached as the gospel of Wall Street for the past fifty years has, in my mind, become an invitation to a game of chance. If you get lucky—really lucky—and the markets eventually rebound, achieving an upward climb over the long term, you might have a comfortable retirement. Look closely, however, and you will see a disclaimer printed on almost every piece of financial literature or advertisement: "Past performance is no guarantee of future results." So much for the idea that stocks *always* go up.

Each year millions of Americans are unwittingly taken for a ride on this risk roller coaster, either on their own or at the advice of an advisor. To be fair, I truly believe the vast majority of advisors have good intentions, and many are well trained and passionate about their work and their clients. The problem is twofold: First, the traditional, mainstream financial services industry has not yet created product solutions designed to work in protracted down or flat markets. Second, starting in their "Introduction to Finance" class in college, many advisors are taught to focus on the client's portfolio instead of the client, the means rather than the end. Were they taught to view the world of investing from a more holistic point of view, perhaps they would take into consideration the real priorities of many retirees: (1) producing sufficient cash flow to enjoy their lifestyle no matter what and (2) protecting their assets from a potential catastrophic event such as a lawsuit.

In the course of my profession, I have had the privilege of meeting a number of individual investors with net worths that cover a broad spectrum. Although some of the people I have met may enjoy the occasional adrenaline rush that comes with rolling the dice, I have never met anyone who was comfortable taking a serious risk with the money they needed to make the mortgage payment or pay their health insurance premiums. I have found that many people just want to be able to work hard, save diligently, and do what is necessary to create and sustain a certain type of lifestyle.

This brings us to an important two-part question that I hear from nearly all of my clients: How much is enough, and when do I know I can retire? As you might guess, the answer involves more than just a magic number. It's an entire process, beginning with a very personal look at the kind of lifestyle you hope to enjoy. That process is the subject of this book.

In the next chapter, I will show you why certain methods you may be using are flawed and, more significantly, why they are not likely to work in the future. In today's economic environment, creating the retirement you've always dreamed about will require some new learning. You'll need to know what won't work every bit as much as you'll need to know what will work. It will require adopting an entirely new philosophy about money—and the longer you wait for the old, traditional methods to start working again, the more you stand to lose.

ERIN'S ESSENTIALS

- Many of the tenets Wall Street has been heralding for years are actually myths, and an investment strategy built around them may be a set up for disaster. Here are the four most common myths as I see them:

  - *In the long term, the stock market always goes up.* My question to you is, as a retiree, do you have enough time before you run out of money to wait for things to go back up?

  - *Diversification and asset allocation are the keys to investment success.* They are ways to reduce overall risk, but there is still a major disconnect between how money is invested and how much income it takes to pay a retiree's monthly bills.

  - *Investing through a major financial services firm gives you more options.* The truth is, you may receive flashier presentations but often more "vanilla" investment choices, especially when it comes to income-producing opportunities.

  - *Your net worth determines your lifestyle in retirement.* This all depends on whether you can convert your net worth into income-producing vehicles to pay your bills.

- **Ask yourself:** Is my financial future based on something that may be a myth?

For more information and complimentary reports, go to **www.thebigretirementrisk.com.**

CHAPTER 3

WHY TRADITIONAL METHODS AREN'T RELIABLE

For the past thirty years, the financial services industry has promoted methods of creating retirement income that have worked in some cases and not in others. If you follow their traditional advice, what will your outcome be? Will it work or not work? I assume you'd like to be on the winning side of that question.

Unfortunately, not much has changed in the mainstream investment world during the last thirty years. The old methods are still being used and promoted as if their failures in recent years never happened. Far worse, the industry has attempted to become ever more precise even while using these flawed tools. They now have computer simulation programs that make sophisticated calculations to create an "optimized portfolio." When all of the data is entered, you are given a report that says something like "Mr. Client, if we optimize your portfolio, according to our formulas, you will have a 91 percent chance of never running out of money." And that is supposed to make you feel good.

For all of these elegant formulas to work, there are certain basic assumptions about the economy and the financial markets that have to be true. Some of these assumptions are that

- The stock market, while often volatile in the short run, has a relatively predictable upward bias.
- If you are a long-term investor, you can base your future on some "average" annual return. I have often seen 10 percent used as the assumption for an average annual return for stock portfolios.
- Stocks, over the long term, will always outperform bonds.
- Real estate should form the basis of one's net worth since real estate, for the most part, has always gone up in value.

Many of you probably know from personal experience that these assumptions are not always true. In order to see just how devastating they can be when used as the basis for a retiree's financial plan, let's take a closer look at how these traditional methods work—or potentially *don't* work.

THE TRADITIONAL CRAPSHOOT

The four biggest problems with traditional asset allocation methods are described in the following list:

1. They are backward looking. They are based on historical data that normally includes the period during which 77 million baby boomers in their peak earning and spending years had a significant impact on the economy and the financial markets. For example, to include figures of the stock market

during the "go-go '90s" in your retirement planning would be to inflate the returns a reasonable person should actually expect to receive during retirement.

2. Because the models are not forward-looking, they cannot anticipate these 77 million baby boomers going over the hill and what changes that will mean for the economy and the financial markets. They do not account for the fact that many of these people will be out of the workforce, spending less money, and will eventually die. They also do not account for the obvious supply-and-demand issue of more money being taken out of the financial markets than the next generation is putting in.

3. These models assume the rational behavior of the financial markets when, in fact, we know markets do not behave rationally. In a rational market, events in a small, faraway country would not cause the biggest stock market in the world to fall by nearly 10 percent. Yet we have seen this happen. There is also the issue of investor sentiment, which can swing like a pendulum from extreme greed to extreme fear. Of course, these fears do not have to be rational at all. When the collective masses get scared, they sell. Mathematical formulas certainly cannot anticipate this kind of behavior or account for the psychology of the masses.

4. Traditional asset allocation models make no distinction between someone who retires at the peak of a market cycle (think of those retiring in 1999) versus the person who retires and has cash to invest at the bottom of a market cycle (as in 2003). To see just how significant even the difference of a year can be, look at the following comparison of two investors.

Jonathan Smith

Retires December 1972.

Has $250,000 invested in the S&P 500, with a 5 percent withdrawal per year.

Jonathan received $413,000 of income.

Jonathan runs out of money in 1989, just seventeen years later.

William Reynolds

Retires December 1973 (one year after Jonathan).

Has $250,000 invested in the S&P 500, with a 5 percent withdrawal per year.

William received $1,166,000 of income ($750,000 more than Jonathan).

Account worth $859,000 on December 31, 2006, thirty-three years later.

In the comparison, Jonathan retired and invested his money in the S&P 500 at the peak of a market cycle. The market went down dramatically right after he retired, causing him to burn through his savings in just seventeen years. William was fortunate enough to retire and invest his money one year later at the bottom of a market cycle. His portfolio grew from there, allowing him to increase his withdrawals and still maintain an impressive investment base even after thirty-three years. Pretty remarkable, isn't it? One year can make a huge difference.

In my mind, using traditional forms of asset allocation and retirement planning are, at best, a total crapshoot. For some, using these assumptions and methods might work out, like it did for William. For others, like Jonathan, it will be a complete disaster. Why risk it?

Let's go back and use the traditional assumption that over the long haul the stock market has a reasonable chance of returning an average of 10 percent. Remember Myth #1, "In the long term, the stock market always goes up"? That assumption clearly did not take into account the following years that were also illustrated in living color in the previous chapter as Figure 2.1:

- From 1906 to 1924, a period of eighteen years, the market was flat.
- From 1929 to 1954, a period of twenty-five years, the market was flat.
- From 1965 to 1982, a period of seventeen years, the market was flat.
- From 2000 to 2010, a period of ten years, the market was flat.

Had you invested at the beginning of any of these cycles, you may have had quite a different outcome than the one you expected. The question is, "How can you plan for your future lifestyle needs by investing in a market that operates like this?"

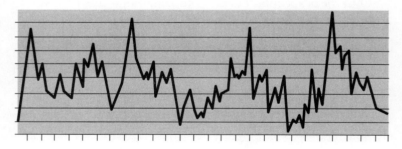

Figure 3.1

My answer is, "You *can't.*"

As humans, we tend to focus on recent events and outcomes and think these outcomes are now the new norm. Many boomers fondly remember the stunning stock market returns they received in the 1990s, particularly from 1995 to 2000. We came to expect those double-digit returns and were very upset if we didn't receive them.

Take the story of a former client whom I'll call "Edna." Edna came to me in 1995 at the beginning of a raging bull market. Everything was going up, and she was living off the alimony from her divorce while she watched her portfolio grow. Her alimony, however, was going to last only ten years, at which point she would need to live off her portfolio. But in 1999, at the height of the tech boom, Edna's greed got the best of her. Despite my words of caution, she demanded that we put all of her money into technology stocks. She was seeing her friends make a killing off their tech-heavy portfolios and wanted a bigger piece of the pie. After numerous discussions, I realized Edna and I no longer shared the same investment philosophy, and I had to let her go as a client. We parted ways amicably, and she took her portfolio to someone who allowed her to pool all her money into tech stocks.

Over the next couple of years, the technology-laden NASDAQ went down almost 90 percent. Though I never heard from her again, it's not hard to surmise what happened. My guess is that the "tech wreck" of 2000 destroyed Edna's portfolio, likely leaving her flat broke once she stopped receiving her alimony checks.

When we let greed dominate our thought processes, we usually don't end up making great decisions. Edna's greed ultimately destroyed her chances of living a comfortable lifestyle. But it isn't always greed; I see other clients whose investment philosophies are dictated by fear. They are so fearful of making decisions that they do nothing and miss out on wonderful opportunities. These people allow fear to impact their ability to enjoy the lifestyle they have worked so hard to achieve. Greed and fear are probably the two most dangerous emotions when mixed with your investment strategy.

Edna's story is a good reminder that the stock market doesn't always go up; in fact, there are sometimes multiple years when it goes down. For many people, those tech-wreck years from 2000 to 2003 were a game changer. People who retired before the crash and followed traditional forms of asset allocation found themselves in a vastly different place than they had anticipated.

However, traditional asset allocation does not fail all of the time. And that is what makes it so frustrating. Over certain periods it has worked splendidly, completely achieving its goal of delivering respectable returns. The problem is that it simply isn't reliable, which can clearly be a problem for retirees. And of course there are times, such as in 2008, when it breaks down completely.

"Well, nothing is perfect, but asset allocation usually works" is a reply I often hear in the industry. That might be so, but "usually works" is not much consolation to the couple who sees their retirement dreams vanish during one of the times when it doesn't work.

THE RECENCY BIAS

Even if asset allocation works some of the time, there is another problem that goes deeper. Asset allocation is fundamentally contrary to the way we humans think and is thus very hard to actually use. Our brains take certain mental shortcuts that lead to what behavioral economists call "heuristic-driven biases."

One of these biases is the recency bias, which means that our brains tend to put undue importance on recent events. What this means in the world of investing is that we are inclined to believe that recent events—like stock market gains or losses—will continue into the future, even if taking a more historical or realistic view would prove the contrary.

So when it comes to asset allocation, we are hardwired to do the exact opposite of what we should. We buy stocks after they have already risen, which is exactly the time we should be selling them, and then we sell out of fear when prices fall, theoretically the best time to buy.

Let me show you how the traditional asset allocation model was meant to be used. We'll start with a hypothetical $1-million portfolio with a target allocation of 60 percent stocks and 40 percent bonds.

Account Value:	$1,000,000
Stocks:	$600,000
Bonds:	$400,000

This is a simplistic view of a traditionally allocated portfolio, but hopefully you'll get the gist.

During a big boom, where the stock market soars and the bond market is flat, here's what might happen:

> The stock portfolio goes up 25 percent to $750,000.
> The bond portfolio stays stable at $400,000.
> The total is now $1,150,000.

The portfolio is up 15 percent on average. That's good news. To maintain the discipline of traditional asset allocation, however, you should, on a quarterly or an annual basis, go in and rebalance your portfolio to maintain your original 60:40 ratio, which with our example would look as follows:

Total:	$1,150,000
Stocks:	$690,000
Bonds:	$460,000

In this case, you would need to sell off $60,000 of your impressively performing stock portfolio and add it to your bond portfolio (which in your mind wasn't doing anything) in order to maintain your supposed "risk adjusted" allocation. Unfortunately, many people fail to complete this step.

During the late 1990s, many people convinced themselves not to rebalance their portfolios. The arguments and logic behind this decision were actually very interesting. The vast majority of investors had convinced themselves that somehow it was different this time, that we were living in a "new economy," and that technology had changed the rules of investing forever. When the market collapsed in the period between 2000 and 2003, those who had failed to rebalance their portfolios by selling stocks and buying bonds also failed to lock in any of their prior gains. As a result, much of what they had earned just slipped away.

CASH FLOW IS KING

Even if asset allocation works during the accumulation stage of your working years and you manage to keep your nest egg intact, the methods for converting that nest egg into actual income to fund your retirement needs are at best flawed and at worst nonexistent. The models don't take into consideration the one thing the vast majority of retirees need, which is cash flow.

Traditional models of asset allocation don't take into consideration the one thing the vast majority of retirees need: cash flow.

Instead, traditional asset allocation models are built around ridiculous formulas such as this: "To decide how much you should have in stocks versus bonds, take 100 and subtract your age. That's the percentage you should have in stocks." What? How in the world does that formula equate to paying your mortgage and electric bills? If you were seventy years old and had $1 million, this formula would say you should have $700,000 in bonds or cash and $300,000 in stocks. Let's assume the bond and cash portfolio gave you an average income of 4 percent, or $28,000, and the stock portion produced no income. Is that the amount of cash flow you need?

Well, it depends. Does that number, along with your Social Security or pension check, add up to the amount you need to pay your mortgage and electric bills and buy food? If it does, great; you have your bases covered. If not, then can you see the problem with this formula? It is based on some arbitrary number using your age, not a real number using the actual total of your monthly expenses.

Realizing that the vast majority of models would not provide sufficient cash flow for the average retiree, financial planners had to create some sort of work-around. One popular solution was the method of using systematic withdrawals from balanced port-folios to pay yourself an income once a month. This was the most widely used method among retiree investors, and it worked pretty well—as long as the markets were going up. Needless to say, it didn't work quite so well *after* the markets peaked in 2000, and it certainly didn't work well during 2008.

This method of using systematic withdrawals from balanced portfolios was analogous to dollar-cost-averaging into the markets, which many of us did for years as we accumulated our net worth by putting regular, systematic investments into our retirement plans over time. Instead of dollar-cost-averaging into the markets, systematic withdrawals effectively would dollar-cost-average us *out* of the market by selling small pieces of our portfolio each month to be withdrawn and spent.

This model works fine—as long as the market is rising faster than you are withdrawing. If the market is returning 10 percent per year and you are spending only 5 percent, then your portfolio will actually grow. But what happens if the market return is less than your withdrawal rate? Or, even worse, what if the market is negative?

When we were in the accumulation time of our life, we didn't mind the down times in the markets. In fact, if we were smart, we relished the opportunities to buy more shares at lower prices. Some of us even chose to double up on our investments during these times because we knew we had a limited amount of time to capture these low points in the markets. After all, the stock market always goes up over time, doesn't it?

As history shows, the market doesn't always have an upward bias. It soon became clear for retirees that using systematic withdrawals during a bear market was a recipe for disaster. Retirees who depended on this strategy ran the real risk of running out of money before they ran out of time.

POTENTIAL BLACK SWAN EVENTS

Thus far I have made the argument that traditional asset allocation methods are flawed primarily because they are based on unrealistic expectations. They fail to consider the very real retirement need for cash flow, and they make no allowance for prolonged bear markets or even swift, violent crashes. But there is another reason these strategies won't work: they do not allow for "Black Swan" events.

Along my path as a financial advisor, there have been many market-savvy people who have influenced how I think about money. One was Nassim Nicholas Taleb, author of the books *Fooled by Randomness* and *The Black Swan*.

Taleb popularized the term "Black Swan event," a metaphor that originally came from the work of the philosopher Karl Popper. Popper made the observation that you can observe a million swans that are white and draw the conclusion that all swans are white, but it takes the sighting of just one black swan to prove your theory completely wrong. Europeans believed that all swans were white because they had never observed a black one—until British sailors spotted black swans in Australia during the colonial period. Sound familiar? It's like saying stocks *always* return 10 percent—until they don't. Or like assuming systematic withdrawals of 4 to 5 percent will *always* allow a retiree to enjoy a good lifestyle without dipping too heavily into the principal—until the market unexpectedly drops by 50 percent.

Compare this to managing a mutual fund or hedge fund. For years, journalists at the *Wall Street Journal* threw darts at a dartboard to select stocks at random. Quite regularly, the dartboard stocks beat the vast majority of mutual funds. How many hot fund managers have we seen spectacularly blow up over the years, particularly in the 2008 meltdown? Could it be that their initial success was more attributable to luck than skill? As I like to say, don't confuse brains with a bull market!

My intention is not to beat up on mutual fund managers and hedge fund managers. There are plenty of talented managers out there who do very well for their investors. But to be sure, luck does play a significant role in the world of finances, and we are all too often fooled by randomness. We have to remain cautiously skeptical when presented with information that seemingly explains away market activities, for in many cases, the market reaction is far more random than rational. And if the market is more random than rational, that should be at least a little bit scary to the average retiree. It is to me!

Luck plays a significant role in the world of finances, and we are all too often fooled by randomness.

Perhaps the biggest risk to us as investors today is what Taleb calls the "ludic fallacy," or the temptation to quantify everything in precise numbers. The belief that risk is no longer a concept, that it can be expressed as a number, leads to a false sense of security as we rely on a degree of precision that simply isn't there.

Think about the subprime mortgage disaster that began in 2008. Banks took far more risk than they should have by lending far too much money on inflated properties to borrowers who often lacked the means to pay. Why? Because their risk models told them it was okay.

Similarly, how many hedge funds blew up during the 2008 crisis? The traders were far more aggressive than they should have been because their elaborate risk models gave them a false sense of security. Models, of course, are only as good as their inputs. You put garbage in, you will get garbage out. It really doesn't matter how elegant the formulas are.

Legendary value investor Benjamin Graham focused on determining a margin of safety in his investments and passed that wisdom on to his protégé, Warren Buffett. Buffett jokes that he likes his investments to wear both a belt and suspenders. Because you can never fully know the future or take all risks into account, you need that all-important margin of safety, which is all too lacking in modern financial theory.

This brings us back to the Black Swan metaphor, which has slipped into everyday speech by now. In Taleb's words, a Black Swan event is a low-probability, high-impact event. By nature, it is very unpredictable and virtually impossible to accurately calculate the odds of one occurring. But when it happens, it can have a catastrophic impact on a large number of people. For example, September 11, 2001, was a Black Swan event. No one had ever committed a terrorist act by flying a plane into a skyscraper, so it never occurred to Americans to be prepared for it. The tsunami of 2004 that hit Southeast Asia was also a Black Swan event. Similarly, the 2011 earthquake in Japan had significant and unexpected ramifications for the global economy and stock markets. How do you calculate the odds of something like that happening?

Taleb later infers that some Black Swan events represent huge opportunities as well. The creation of the computer was that sort of opportunity. So, to be sure, these highly improbable and highly unpredictable events need not only be tragedies; they can be marvels too. According to Taleb, you just need to be in a financial position to be able to take advantage of them. Once you have your basic lifestyle needs met and have plenty of cash flow, there can be opportunities to participate in positive Black Swan events.

After studying Taleb's work, I have come to the following conclusions: We have no way of knowing how many more Black Swan events may occur in the future; after all, if we could anticipate them, they would not be considered Black Swans. What we do know is that because of the Internet, traders and market speculators find out about global incidents instantaneously and can act on a dime to buy and sell securities in large volumes. Let's face it—the large institutional traders move the markets, not you and me. They are trading in very large volumes and hence any large trade can cause significant volatility in their respective markets.

As we all know, the United States economy is interconnected with the broader global economy, as the process of globalization has integrated the world economy like never before. Regardless of where something happens, it can have an instantaneous impact on the global economy. We saw this happen during the financial crisis of 2008, and it has continued since then. The U.S. financial crisis wreaked havoc in Europe, and the near bankruptcies of the countries that are referred to as the PIIGS—Portugal, Ireland, Italy, Greece, and Spain—created quite a stir in the U.S.

markets as well. As of this writing, the long-term impact these overleveraged countries will have on the world economic platform is uncertain.

But what does this mean to you? And perhaps more importantly, what should you do about it? It means you will need a new way to think about money and investing in order to protect your lifestyle in up *and* down markets and to capitalize on opportunities in the marketplace as they present themselves.

You now know why traditional methods of asset allocation and retirement income planning will not likely work for retirees in the days ahead. Add to that my belief that we will have much more volatility in our markets in the future and you could have a recipe for financial disaster, especially for retirees. This is why it is imperative for us to stop using the old tools—or, at the very least, to change the *way* we use them—as we shift to a new paradigm for the new economy.

Before we jump into how the new paradigm should look, let's take a minute to examine the factors that *do* drive the economy and how they should influence your planning.

ERIN'S ESSENTIALS

- You can't plan for your future if your investment strategy is built on hope and high "probabilities of success." Mathematical models aren't an accurate predictor of retirement success.
- Traditional methods assume things about the financial markets that, if they don't work out, can decimate an asset allocation portfolio. For instance, they assume the markets will, at some point, return to an upward bias.
  - **Question:** If you are retired and pulling money out of your balanced portfolio, will you have anything left if and when the markets finally turn around?
- For a retiree, relying solely on asset allocation, diversification, and a systematic withdrawal program can have disastrous consequences in years when the markets go down several years in a row.
  - **Question:** How many years does the market have to go down by 30 percent or more before you run out of money?
- **Ask yourself:** The world is changing faster than ever—is my investment strategy changing with it or am I relying on methods from the past?

For more information and complimentary reports, go to
www.thebigretirementrisk.com.

CHAPTER 4

UNDERSTANDING WHAT DRIVES THE ECONOMY

Until you understand what drives the overall economy, you will be at the mercy of views and illustrations of the markets prepared by others, which can be contrived to show you optimal times in the past. This brings to mind a little nugget of wisdom from Mark Twain: "Figures don't lie, but liars figure."

When financial planners base future projections on historical examples, even with the best of intentions, it is like driving while looking through the rearview mirror! It might work fine as long as the road is perfectly straight, but if the financial markets become volatile you could end up driving your perfect retirement over the proverbial cliff.

The power the baby boom generation has had on the economy in the past cannot be overstated. That generation has been likened to a pig passing through a python, and for good reason. It has completely dominated the American consumer culture for decades. The question is, when all those boomers go over the hill or quit spending or, worse yet, die, then what happens to the economy and the markets?

Keep in mind that I was originally trained by the "system." Having a business degree from a major university and going through a traditional stockbroker training program, I was taught that as long as our society was based on capitalism and backed up by democracy, our economy would always grow and the next generation in our country would live better than the last.

Interestingly enough, this financial myth also engendered the belief that the stock market would always go up—*eventually.* From my early days as a broker, a common mantra was "the stock market climbs a wall of worry." Somehow that saying was supposed to give both our clients and us comfort. Not only were we taught to believe the stock market would always go up, somewhere along the line our entire generation came to believe it was our birthright that real estate would always appreciate, our savings would always grow, our futures would be safe, and we were all entitled to a comfortable retirement. Oh, how I loved those promises!

Even having grown up in poverty, I had no reason to question that this was the way things were supposed to be. In fact, these ideas gave me hope for a better future. The American Dream actually gave me the license to presume I would never be poor again and my life would be a fairy tale of economic comfort and financial security.

This belief system was present in our country for decades. Then, too, it was fueled by a force so big it propelled our economy upward with seemingly no end in sight. That force was the power of the 77 million babies that made up the baby boom generation. In 1995, when I began my more intentional, in-depth study of the economy and the financial markets, I had no idea how integral this force would be to our future economic landscape. But I was about to find out.

THE FIRST STORM CLOUD: DEMOGRAPHICS

Just like the thermometer we use to measure our temperature and health, the financial markets—such as the stock, bond, and real estate markets—are somewhat like temperature gauges that measure the health of our economy. So what determines the health of our economy? Put simply, it is *spending* that drives our economy and consumer spending in particular that accounts for approximately 70 percent of our economic activity, as measured by a calculation called the gross domestic product.

Think about it this way. Consumers spend money to buy something—a good or a service. The companies providing the good or service create profits from that spending and, if they are public companies, report those profits every quarter as earnings. Normally, the price of the underlying stock will follow the earnings.

People spend money.
Spending creates profits.
Profits are reported as earnings.
Stock prices follow earnings.

This information begs the question, who is doing all the spending? My original research in 1995 started with the work of

Harry S. Dent Jr., founder of the H.S. Dent Foundation, an organization with the mission of helping people understand demographic shifts and changes. Dent studied and documented how and when Americans purchase everything from toothpaste and speedboats, designer shoes and vacation homes, to cellular phones and cellophane. He then compiled peak spending charts based on age for literally hundreds of products.

Looking for a tool he could use to measure overall economic activity, Dent averaged terabytes of data to find out that, in aggregate, we reach our peak spending years between the ages of forty-six and fifty, or age forty-eight on average. This will probably not surprise parents, but this age generally coincides with when our children start to leave the nest. From there, as we age, our spending tends to decline. From this research, Dent derived the graph in Figure 4.1.

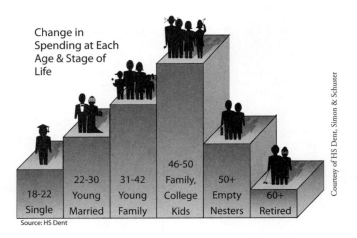

Figure 4.1: Spending by Age

Since he knew how much money people spent on various products by age, Dent combined that information with the *number* of people at each age, creating a powerful tool that forecasts demand for those products.

The U.S. National Center for Health Statistics publishes the number of live births in the United States every year. Dent combined this information with immigration data from the Immigration and Naturalization Service, made his own estimates for future immigration, and came up with The Immigration-Adjusted Birth Index (Figure 4.2).

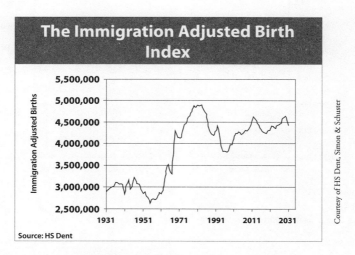

Figure 4.2: The Immigration-Adjusted Birth Index

Since spending is a huge driver of the economy, Dent decided to see if there was any correlation between the number of peak spenders (forty-eight-year-olds) and the stock market. In order to do this, he added forty-eight years to the graph of the immigration-adjusted birth index and overlaid it with a graph of the Dow Jones Industrial Average, adjusted for inflation. The resulting graph shows what Dent calls "The Spending Wave" (Figure 4.3). It's no coincidence that the peak spenders and the Dow are nearly identical images.

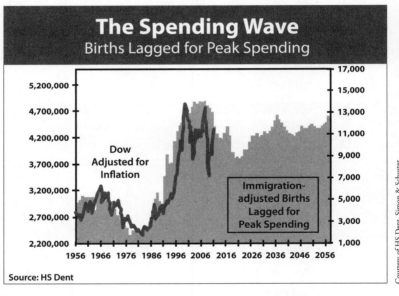

Figure 4.3: The Spending Wave from 1956 to 2056

Figure 4.3 shows that the number of forty-eight-year-olds and the stock market both hit a peak in 2008. This graph projects economic data into the future by showing the number of forty-eight-year-olds who will be living in the United States through 2056.

This information is important because, as demographer Phillip Longman put it, "Demographics are the future that has

already been written." Fewer peak spenders in the years to come
will mean less spending, which doesn't bode well for our economy. If spending is indeed a factor in our economic landscape, we
have now begun the long downhill slide of the spending curve.
While consumer spending is just one of the many factors that
could affect our economic future, the power of consumer spending on our overall economy cannot be overstated. That being said,
according to birth rates, the demographic wave should subside
and start going back up in the mid-2020s as the large generation
that comes after us goes into their peak spending years. The question you must ask yourself is this: "If the markets stay flat or go
down between now and then, and if, during that time, I will have
had to start tapping into my investment portfolio, will I run out
of money before the markets have a chance to turn around?"

Since the housing market is an even more important indi-
cator of a country's overall economic health, Dent predicted in
one study that the peak of the U.S. residential real estate market
would occur sometime around the year 2003. How did he know
this? In his studies, he determined that peak spending for housing actually occurs at the age of forty-two versus forty-eight for
overall spending. The peak birth year during the original postwar
baby boom was 1961. If you add those two numbers together
(42 and 1961) you arrive at the year 2003, which corresponds
well to the peak year for "McMansion" home buying. Do you
think it is a coincidence that the housing bubble really started to
take off at that time? Is it really any surprise the housing decline
began in 2005 and went downhill from there? The demographic
forces pushing the housing market higher peaked in 2003. Only
wild speculation and the most lax lending standards in history

allowed the bubble to keep rising for an additional two years, with predictable results.

This economic data is not all bad news. In fact, there will be companies that do well despite the lower spending by this generation. For example, companies that cater to new parents should do comparatively well as the children of the baby boomers are now having children of their own in record numbers. There is also a very valid argument that the boomer generation will begin spending money on other needs such as health care and retirement housing. I have heard it said, "If you want to get rich, just stay ten years ahead of the baby boom generation and create products they need." Companies that continue to anticipate where boomers will be spending money stand to profit.

There have been and still are many financial pundits who continue to argue that the demographic argument has no validity, but I am grateful I had the opportunity to see this body of work as far back as 1995. Until that time, I was aware of only one school of thought: the markets would always go up—*eventually*. Certainly the powers on Wall Street wanted us to believe the myth; it didn't benefit them to have investors think anything else. If people stopped investing in Wall Street's equity mutual funds or other forms of stock portfolios, a lot of people on Wall Street potentially could lose their jobs, and the house of cards that was beginning to form could tumble.

Seeing the demographic evidence made me realize there was a strong possibility the Wall Street message could one day be wrong, and I decided to figure out what to do if that scenario ever became a reality. My goal from the very beginning of this revelation in 1995 was to come up with a set of rules and a philosophy about money that could withstand various scenarios in the economy. Fortunately, since I had found this demographic information early, I had time on my side. The biggest challenge I faced was finding investment vehicles and strategies that were geared to withstand a sideways or down economy. I spent the next several years searching for products and developing a strategy that would do just that.

Because I did not receive a lot of industry support for my newfound beliefs, I decided to move out of the world of being a stockbroker and become an independent financial advisor. This was a big move back then, but it appeared I was going to be on my own anyway in terms of studying the economy and designing strategies and solutions for my clients.

I committed to show this baby boomer/demographic evidence to every client I worked with from that day forward. Every time I showed these charts I would tell my clients that we can't argue with birth rates in this country or the demographic statistics because they are a matter of public record. The baby boom generation does exist and is a powerful force in our economy. There is nothing we can do to change this; we must simply be aware of it and respond accordingly. Fortunately, our Lifestyle Driven Investing philosophy was created and refined to help protect our clients' lifestyles from what appeared to be the inevitable, namely, a slowing economy and a potentially protracted period of lackluster stock market performance.

If the aging of America and the seismic demographic shift isn't enough to challenge the economy, there is clear evidence of more storm clouds on the horizon that could negatively impact the financial markets. My point in continuing this discussion is not to belabor the negativity but to deal with the reality of our times.

THE SECOND STORM CLOUD: THE STATE OF PENSIONS AND SOCIAL SECURITY

In our parents' day, the companies they worked for provided for them in their retirement. Companies contributed to pension plans, and they guaranteed that retirees would receive a monthly check for as long as they lived. That was then. In the 1980s, there were 112,000 pension plans still in operation in the United States. By the mid-2000s, there were fewer than 30,000—a drop of 75 percent. So, instead of companies managing pension assets and providing for workers during retirement, they shifted the responsibility, and in effect the risk, to the employees through non-guaranteed, self-managed accounts.

Even if you are fortunate enough to work for a company that still has a pension plan, you might want to look at your employer's annual report a little more closely. The better-known companies in the S&P 500 are operating pension plans that are seriously underwater, and as the baby boomer retirement wave kicks into full gear, this problem will only get worse—a lot worse. In fact, *The S&P 500 2009: Pensions and Other Post-Employment Benefits* published in July 2010 by S&P Indices shows that in the year 2009, aggregate pension assets of the S&P 500 were $261 billion short of pension liabilities. Only 18 companies out of the 500 in the index had pensions that were fully funded. According to a recent Mercer Study, a full 13 percent of the S&P 500 companies' pension plans are in the "most serious" risk-exposure category. And all this is happening right on the cusp of the biggest retirement wave in the history of the world. This doesn't bode well for the retirees or the companies.

Many private pensions are at least partially insured by the Pension Benefit Guaranty Corporation (PBGC), a U.S. government entity that was put in place to back pension plans should a company default on their promises. The problem is that the insurer itself is in trouble! This government-run program was underfunded by $21.9 billion as of their fiscal year ending in 2009. According to The Brookings Institute, the PBGC could eventually be underwater by more than $100 billion unless the fund begins taking in substantially larger premiums.

And the states? Their situations are not any better. State pensions went from being substantially overfunded during the dotcom boom of the late 1990s to being severely underfunded today. A report published by Wilshire Consulting on February 28, 2011, estimates that 99 percent of state pension plans are underfunded, with an average funding ratio of only 66 percent. These estimates are based on 2010 reported actuarial data from ninety-nine state retirement systems across all fifty states. The short version: state pensions are in serious trouble as well.

Federal entitlement programs are no better. Social Security is in the same situation, but on a much larger scale. It, too, is already critically underfunded as it enters into a phase of heavy liabilities with the retiring baby boomer wave. In 1940 there were sixteen workers supporting each retiree. By 1970 that number had fallen to just three and a half workers per retiree. And by 2030 just over two workers will be supporting each retiree. That's your son and your daughter working to fund the retirement of someone they've never met.

But what about the Social Security Trust Fund? Surely there is money socked away somewhere, right? I hate to be a cynic, but the so-called Social Security Trust Fund is one of the biggest lies ever told to us by our leaders. There is no "trust fund" in the way many of us understand the term, but instead a large collection of IOUs. Let me explain.

Social Security has been running a surplus for decades—this is the good news. However, the surplus is not sitting in a big account somewhere. Instead, excess Social Security funds are used to buy government bonds, and the money is ultimately used to fund various government programs. This means the government has effectually been borrowing from the Social Security Trust Fund to get cheap financing for its deficits. By government estimates, the Social Security surplus turns to a deficit in 2014. This means that rather than being a source of cheap funding for the government, Social Security is about to become a very large expense—to a country with a budget that can't afford it.

No matter how you spin it, the numbers didn't work in 1970, they don't work now, and they aren't going to work in 2030. When the largest generation in history retires, there simply will not be enough cash in this system to support it.

What does this mean for you? Unfortunately, there are limited ways to fix Social Security. Retirees can either be paid less or workers can be taxed more—or some combination of the two. According to William G. Shipman, chairman of the Cato Institute Project on Social Security Choice, neither of these options really addresses the root problem of Social Security—its pitifully low "investment" returns. Because benefits are linked to wages, which increase about 1.5 percent per year, benefits increase at about the same rate.

Of course, the only way Social Security can achieve higher returns is by taking some amount of risk in the capital markets. After the chaos of 2008, that's not a particularly attractive option either.

One final option—though completely unfair to those of us who saved and invested wisely—would be to conduct a means test of Social Security pensioners. This would mean that if you have other sources of retirement income, you would likely not get your full Social Security benefits. Rather than being a retirement program, it could become a welfare program.

Think it can't happen? Remember, Social Security is not a constitutional guarantee, nor is it even technically a contractual guarantee like many private pensions. Congress created Social Security and Congress can alter it.

Bottom line: You *might* get to enjoy full Social Security benefits, but it is certainly not a guarantee. And the wealthier you are, the less likely you are to receive benefits. My advice to you is to hope for the best but plan for the worst.

THE THIRD STORM CLOUD: HEALTH CARE

Just as this behemoth group of baby boomers will retire and need money to live on, they will also require more health care than any other generation in history. In keeping with the trend of government-run programs, health benefits are also severely underfunded. They are so underfunded, in fact, that it makes the money problems plaguing pensions and Social Security look like a walk in the park.

Like Social Security, Medicare functions as a pay-as-you-go system. Claims are paid as they come in, and this works well so long as there are enough workers to keep contributing to stay ahead of the claims. But when the number of claimants increases, the number and size of the claims will increase too. This will happen at precisely the same time the number of workers who can contribute to the health care pool begins declining. When you combine the unfunded Social Security and Medicare liabilities, you get an almost unbelievable $46 trillion in unfunded liabilities (see Figure 4.4). It makes our current budget deficit look like pocket change by comparison.

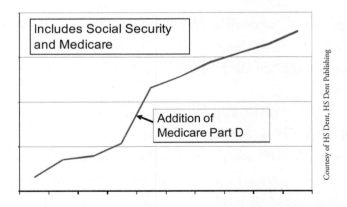

Figure 4.4: Unfunded Entitlement Obligations in Trillions

It's worth mentioning, but I won't belabor the point, that there are other health care storm clouds brewing as well: the trends of rising costs and shortages of care, unchecked malpractice lawsuits, the costs of medical school, a pill with a price for every ailment, and the list goes on. Those factors weigh into this equation too.

PREPARE FOR THE WORST, HOPE FOR THE BEST, SEIZE OPPORTUNITIES

Before you start thinking I'm an eternal pessimist, let me tell you I am not. I truly do hope for the best. I hope the aging baby boom generation and concurrent reduction in spending has no negative impact on our economy. I hope the Social Security system pulls through and the full benefit is available for me, my son, and my future grandkids. I hope Medicare is available for those who need it and health care costs in general do not skyrocket. I hope for all of these things to happen, I just don't stake my financial future on the assumption that they will. I would much rather be prepared for the worst-case scenario and be pleasantly surprised if things turn out better than that.

We live in an interesting world in an interesting time. I believe we need to go back to the basics and focus first on securing what we can in terms of our lifestyles. It is my belief that once you have your basic lifestyle locked down and/or secured, it allows you to use the rest of your money to take advantage of other opportunities, such as investments in new ideas and companies that could be the next Microsoft or Google.

With all of this in mind, are you ready to begin your journey to get ahead of the curve? Are you ready to begin planning your future by looking forward rather than through the rearview mirror of the last thirty years? Knowing the demographic cycle and its potential impact on the financial markets, it's time to begin your journey to lock down your lifestyle. This process is what I refer to as Lifestyle Driven Investing. Let's get started!

ERIN'S ESSENTIALS

- Consumer spending drives the economy.
- The "go-go" decade of the 1990s was not the norm; it was the result of 77 million baby boomers earning and spending substantial amounts of money; they were followed by only 41 million in the next generation.
- Enormous "storm clouds" have and will put high levels of pressure on the U.S. economy:
  - Decreased spending and investing as baby boomers retire and simplify their lives.
  - Entitlement programs such as Medicare and Social Security, which are severely underfunded and unprepared to handle the demand that will come as the baby boom generation retires.
  - Health care, which will likely continue getting more and more expensive.
  - Exorbitant debt levels all over the world, which exceed each country's ability to pay.
- Each of these storm clouds puts downward pressure on the economy—and, concurrently, the financial markets—while at the same time pushing the cost of living higher.
- Any investment plan that assumes a steady upward market trend based on historical data, which includes decades like the 1990s, may be destined for disaster.

- **Ask yourself:** Am I prepared for a market that goes flat or negative for another decade or two?

For more information and complimentary reports, go to **www.thebigretirementrisk.com**.

CHAPTER 5

LIFESTYLE DRIVEN INVESTING: LAYING THE FOUNDATION

In the middle of 2009, a couple in their early sixties (whom I'll call Phil and Silvia) came into my office looking browbeaten and defeated. Their story was classic, similar to the story of thousands of people around the country—all variations on the same theme.

Phil and Silvia were pretty shell-shocked from the events of the previous nine months. Prior to the meltdown of 2008, they told me, they'd had an investment portfolio of approximately $5 million with another financial advisor. It was invested in a typical portfolio of stock and bond mutual funds from which they had been taking systematic withdrawals.

Unfortunately, in March 2009, they had cashed out their entire portfolio, in effect locking in their losses. The amount of investable assets they had leftover was about $2.3 million, what they had when they came to see me. They had been accustomed to living on $250,000 a year from their original $5-million portfolio, which was reasonable by conventional standards. But when they did the math, Phil and Silvia quickly realized how long $2.3 million would last if they continued to take out a quarter of a million dollars a year—certainly not a lifetime.

My least favorite thing to tell clients is that they cannot afford something. I would much rather be able to support all of their hopes and dreams. But it is better to be honest than to risk seeing people run out of money before they run out of time. So I had the horrible job of pointing out the obvious. I had to tell Phil and Silvia they were going to have to substantially reduce their lifestyle to make their money last. Cutting their lifestyle in half was a long way from the dream retirement they had planned.

This story is just one example of the weakness I see in modern financial planning. Put bluntly, the standard methods do not adequately protect investors from running out of money before they run out of time. Fortunately, you do not have to be among those ranks. Instead, I would like to propose my alternative to the traditional methods: Lifestyle Driven Investing.

Lifestyle Driven Investing is a new way to frame your investment options and make decisions based on your own specific lifestyle desires. It is a way to think about money, a strategy to help you categorize your needs and wants and then to use investments that produce predictable cash flow to fund those needs and wants. In this chapter, I will share with you the philosophy behind this strategy and help you take the first step toward creating a portfolio that will help ensure that you do not run out of money before you run out of time.

BUILD YOUR HOUSE OF SECURITY

Perhaps your portfolio, like Phil and Silvia's, has already taken a hit. Or maybe you are hoping to ward off disaster before it strikes. In either case, the important thing is to be honest with yourself. I love the saying I learned from my business coach, Dan Sullivan: "All progress begins by telling the truth." For this process to work, it is imperative to be truthful and realistic about your current situation and goals for the future.

> "All progress begins by telling the truth." —Dan Sullivan

The process begins by dividing your expenses into four categories using a simple framework called the "House of Security," something I got from my good friend Emrich Stellar. The House of Security is pictured in Figure 5.1.

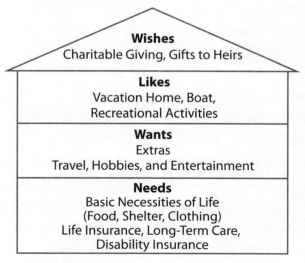

Figure 5.1: The House of Security

The drawing is simple, but the beauty is in its simplicity. In order to construct a house, one must systematically build upon a solid foundation. The foundation of your financial house should be your Needs, and everything else should be built on top. In other words, you cannot start doling out cash for Wants, Likes, and Wishes until you know you have enough to cover the Needs.

Dividing expenses according to this framework will help you look candidly at your finances. And, if you are like many people, you probably fit into one of the following three groups:

1. You may have sufficient resources and have thus far lived within or below your means. If this is the case, begin with the following questions: In your perfect world, what would you want your Preferred Lifestyle to look like? What would you like to be doing after retirement? How do you picture spending your time? If you have plenty of resources, this will probably be a pretty easy and fun exercise. You have the resources to create and maintain a lifestyle that incorporates all of the categories in the House of Security: Needs, Wants, Likes, and Wishes.

2. If your financial resources are not quite as substantial, you will need to make a compromise. You need to determine what truly constitutes a Need, what is a Want, and how a Want is different from a Like. Finally, how do you define a Wish? Regardless of your net worth or the size of your checkbook, you will have your own view of what represents a Need, Want, Like, or Wish. You may want to categorize two vacations per year as a Need. If there are sufficient resources available to allow two vacations a year to be classified as

a Need, I would be the first to support that decision. If there are not, I would be the first to tell you to regroup and reconsider.

3. If you are like some people who are not entirely realistic about their financial resources and the kind of lifestyle those assets will support, then you may need to "back into" the numbers to determine what is realistically possible and what is not.

For instance, I have had a client tell me they want a $300,000-per-year lifestyle, but their assets only support them living on $100,000 per year. Unfortunately, the numbers do not lie. When this happens, I take out the House of Security worksheet and let them plug in their actual lifestyle Needs. Then we go from there. What, beyond their Needs, will that $100,000 support? How many of their Wants, Likes, and Wishes need to be modified?

Obviously, these situations are my least favorite. Unfortunately, I am seeing this outcome more and more because of the financial collapse of 2008 and its serious impact on people nearing retirement. But it isn't the end of the world; it just requires a little creative reworking to get people where they need to go.

START WITH THE BASICS: NEEDS

Regardless of our net worth or the complexity of our finances, we all have fixed bills to pay. A solid financial plan must generate sufficient cash flow to meet the basic necessities of life: a roof over your head and food on the table. Or, as one of my friends says, "three hots and a cot."

Of course, it is a little more complicated than that. To determine the Needs category, you can begin with a basic worksheet. Figure 5.2 outlines what "Eddie and Annie", hypothetical clients—married and in their late fifties—might classify as Needs.

As you can see, there is plenty of room for discussion. For instance, is cable TV or Internet access a Need? In this day and age, many would agree that both *are* Needs. What about dining out? There are definitely some gray areas, and the decision about what to characterize as a Need is different for everyone.

In addition to deciding how much monthly, quarterly, or annual cash flow will be needed to provide for your basic Needs, there are some foundational tools that need to be considered. In no particular order, the following are some examples:

Life Insurance

If you have a spouse or dependents who rely on your income, pension, or anything else that would vanish with your demise, you should have sufficient life insurance to replace that income. In fact, I urge you to make life insurance a foundation of your financial plan.

I know from personal experience how crucial it is to have a good life insurance policy; in fact, I can even be a little militant about it. My father never intended to leave us destitute, but it happened, all because of a lack of planning. I strongly believe that once you bring a child into this world, you have the moral responsibility to make sure that child is cared for, whether or not you are alive. Oftentimes I recommend that retired clients pay for life insurance policies on sons or sons-in-law (or daughters or daughters-in law) to be sure their grandchildren are provided for in case their children die prematurely.

NEEDS		
Personal Residence		
Mortgage/Rent	$	45,600
Property Insurance	$	2,800
Home Maintenance	$	3,000
Property Tax	$	4,950
Groceries	$	6,000
Clothing		
New Purchases	$	4, 000
Dry Cleaning	$	2,600
Medical		
Health Insurance	$	7,200
Deductible	$	800
Prescriptions	$	1,200
Utilities		
Electric/Gas	$	10,200
Telephone	$	600
Cell Phone	$	1,800
Water/Sewer/Garbage	$	480
Cable/Satellite	$	1,320
Internet	$	600
Other	$	–
Transportation		
Car Payment	$	2,400
Auto Insurance	$	2,000
Fuel	$	2,500
Maintenance	$	1,400
Tolls/Parking	$	100
Miscellaneous	$	2, 650
Total Needs	$	**104,200**

Figure 5.2: Eddie and Annie's Needs

Of course, once you are retired and/or have sufficient financial resources to cover your pension or your income, then your overall need for life insurance as an income-replacement tool diminishes. However, it is very rare for me to ever advise someone to give up current life insurance coverage. Life insurance is one of those financial tools that nobody wants until they can't get it. Let me assure you, I have been in plenty of meetings where I had to break the news to people, young and old, that they were uninsurable, and you could have heard a pin drop.

Disability Insurance

Many people have some form of disability insurance through their business or employer. If you do not, you should seriously consider it. Disability insurance is critical while you are working and saving for your future since it is used to replace your income in the event you are unable to work. Once you retire, you are no longer eligible to maintain disability insurance because you are no longer earning income. That's when the next type of foundational insurance becomes vitally important.

Long-term Care Insurance

Our industry used to have some basic standard about who should buy long-term care insurance and who had sufficient financial resources to be considered self-insured. There were many rules of thumb along the way. Some people used to say if someone had a net worth of $5 million or more, they could be considered self-insured. But if a person's net worth consists of assets that do not produce an income—such as vacant land, art, or beachfront property—then no amount of net worth should be considered sufficient self-insurance for long-term care purposes.

I can make the following two arguments about long-term care insurance. If you do not have a lot of resources, then I strongly suggest that you procure long-term care insurance. A major illness that requires nursing home care or home health care could bankrupt you or your family. The worst situation we see is when one spouse uses all of the family resources trying to keep the other spouse alive and then the sick spouse dies, having used the majority of the family resources and thus leaving very little for the survivor to live on.

The second argument may seem like it counters the first, but in reality, both are true. If you do have plenty of resources, then the premiums to secure long-term care insurance are usually low relative to the benefit. In this case, it simply makes good financial sense.

It doesn't matter if you do or do not have substantial resources—long-term care coverage is a wise investment either way. Every retiree or pre-retiree should become educated about this type of insurance. There is obviously a cost involved in securing long-term care coverage, but my belief is that the cost should be considered in the Needs category for many people. However, since there is no cookie-cutter solution, there can always be exceptions.

As you put together your own House of Security, calculate your expenses on a monthly and an annual level, not forgetting commitments that may be due on a different schedule, like a six-month insurance premium. If you are still a number of years from retirement, you may want to factor in inflation that could occur between now and then. Two to three percent is a common baseline assumption, although inflation protection can also be dealt with in the investment products you choose. Any number of resources can be used to account for inflation. For an example, go to our website at www.thebigretirementrisk.com.

BEYOND THE BASICS: WANTS

Differentiating Needs from Wants can be subjective, but it is an important distinction to make if you want to determine how much income you actually *need* as opposed to what you would *prefer*. For example, food would be classified as a Need, but eating out may be considered a Want. The mortgage and utilities on your primary residence are a Need, but the upkeep of a second home might be a Want. The distinction between Needs and Wants becomes important when determining appropriate investments to fund these different categories and your risk tolerance in each area. Figure 5.3 is a list of Eddie and Annie's hypothetical Wants.

CLIMBING THE LADDER: LIKES

Likes are similar to Wants but can include big-ticket items that will require a lump sum of cash to make a large purchase, like a second home, an airplane, or a vacation cruise around the world. However, this category can also include items that require monthly cash flow to maintain.

For instance, if you want to buy a vacation home, it may require a substantial down payment. But the upkeep on that vacation home will certainly require regular, predictable ongoing cash flow. You may classify it as a Like for now, but I would also suggest identifying the amount of cash flow needed to sustain the vacation home and preparing to add that to the Needs category once you make such a purchase. My reasoning is that the upkeep and maintenance is no longer a Like; it is a Need if you do not want to lose that home.

WANTS		
Travel	$	12,000
Hobbies	$	4,500
Entertainment		
Dining Out	$	6,000
Club dues	$	1,060
Recreation	$	1,740
Pets	$	–
Subscriptions	$	200
Other	$	7,200
Personal Care	$	3,900
Other	$	2,000
Total Wants	**$**	**31,400**

Figure 5.3: Eddie and Annie's Wants Worksheet

College education is also an interesting expense. Some people consider the education of their children an absolute Need and put those expenses in this category, while others feel their children should take out student loans to pay for college.

WISHES, OR LEGACY DESIRES— THE ULTIMATE GOAL

Like Maslow's hierarchy of needs, when all of our Needs, Wants, and Likes have been taken care of and our personal life dreams have been fulfilled, there is a higher level of self-actualization that can take place. The ultimate goal of many people is to leave a legacy—evidence they existed other than the tombstone that graces the lawn of a cemetery. When all is said and done, we want our lives to have counted for something. We want to leave something behind that reflects our life's work and our life's purpose. This is why we sometimes call Wishes the "Legacy Desires."

People create a legacy in a variety of ways, but anyone can do it. Regardless of our financial status, all of us have the ability to leave the legacy of character and integrity. Our hope is that our heirs will not remember us for the size of our bank accounts but for the size of our hearts and our impact on the lives of those around us.

However, for those who do have the privilege of making it to the end without running out of money, there are many strategies you can use to ensure that you make the greatest possible financial impact on the next generation. I have been honored to help many people create estate plans that not only leave what they have accumulated to their heirs but also, through innovative estate planning strategies, reduce what eventually gets paid to the government as a death tax.

If you are confident you won't outlive your money, you may consider setting up a family or charitable foundation. There is nothing more exhilarating than realizing the large impact you can have on the next generation without denying yourself the lifestyle you have worked so hard to achieve. Since these estate planning techniques are so personal and varied, I have purposefully left a more thorough discussion of them out of this book in order to focus on the basics of making sure you do not run out of money before you run out of time.

Figure 5.4 is an example of a Likes and Wishes worksheet. I have left this one blank so you can take an unbiased look at your own personal choices in these two categories.

LIKES	
Vacation Home	
Boat	
Recreation	
Education	
Other	
Total Likes	

WISHES	
Heirs	
Charities	
Gifts to Trust	
Other	
Total Wishes	

Figure 5.4: Likes and Wishes Worksheet

The possibilities are exciting. I encourage you to have fun brainstorming your Wishes after your Needs, Wants, and Likes have been met. Building a rich and honorable legacy can be one of the most fulfilling things you ever do.

You have now begun construction on your personal House of Security. Hold on to these numbers because in the next chapter, you're going to put them to good use.

ERIN'S ESSENTIALS

- Any good investment plan must begin by determining the objective you are trying to meet. Otherwise, you have no way of measuring the success of your plan.
- The process of Lifestyle Driven Investing begins by splitting your expenses into four categories ranging from most essential to least essential: Needs, Wants, Likes, and Wishes.
- As you can imagine, different people define Needs and Wants very differently, so this exercise will also tell you something about yourself, your lifestyle, and your investment risk tolerance.
- **Ask yourself:** Some lifestyle expenses clearly have a higher priority than others. Have I ever stopped to prioritize my expenses?

For more information and to get your own House of Security worksheet, go to **www.thebigretirementrisk.com**.

CHAPTER 6

LIFESTYLE DRIVEN INVESTING: CREATING YOUR PREFERRED FUTURE

Many people construct their financial plan without really thinking about where they want to end up; consequently, they often don't have an appropriate strategy to get there. They approach their retirement planning in much the same way Alice, from Lewis Carroll's *Alice in Wonderland*, approached the Cheshire Cat to determine where she should go.

> "Would you tell me, please, which route I ought to go from here?"
>
> "That depends a good deal on where you want to get to," said the Cat.
>
> "I don't much care where," said Alice.
>
> "Then it doesn't matter which way you walk," said the Cat.

In many financial planning offices, the retirement planning process begins with a discussion about investments. But before considering specific strategies or investment products, you must establish what it is you want to achieve. There is no one-size-fits-all model because everyone has different financial resources and different objectives. But there is a framework through which you can determine what is and is not realistically possible for your retirement lifestyle. The five steps described in this chapter will help you lay the groundwork for making investment choices that should assuage your fears about running out of money before you run out of time.

STEP 1: REIGNITE YOUR DREAMS

Lifestyle Driven Investing begins not with esoteric investment concepts but with envisioning the lifestyle you want to create or maintain during your retirement years. Only you can imagine this lifestyle, and you must do more than just fantasize about it. To get your creative mind-set flowing, let's begin by taking a stroll down memory lane.

Once upon a time, when we were young and beginning this journey of life, many of us were pretty idealistic about what our futures would hold. We graduated from high school and perhaps went on to college. Some of us pursued graduate degrees or doctorates; some of us did not. Others went to technical school and learned a specific trade. Many of us got married; some of us did not. Some decided to stay home and raise children, while others pursued careers in the workforce. But somewhere along the line, either by ourselves or with someone else, we had a dream.

This dream was full of hope and promise. Either consciously or subconsciously, we created a bold vision for our future. We had a pretty clear picture of how we wanted to live our lives. At the time—that idealistic, youthful time—our future seemed so clear and so real. We truly believed we could get there. Furthermore, many of us saw our futures as somewhat of a straight line from here to there. It was just time that stood in the way.

Some of us saw things like owning multiple houses. We saw a future life of leisure and seeing the world. Some of us wanted a lake house, a condo at the beach, or a mountain home to get out of the summer heat. We wanted to take care of our families, do mission work, sail around the world, or climb Mt. Everest . . . someday. Oh, how grand a time that would be!

But along came life, and our vision for the future became blurred. We went to work. Our first jobs may not have worked out so well. (I got fired on the first day of my first job!) So we got a second job, or a third, sometimes working multiple jobs to get ahead. Perhaps we started a business. For some of us, being a business owner worked out; for others it didn't, so we went to work for someone else. Some of our marriages lasted, but some of us got divorced. In the course of our work lives, some of us were transferred around the country or around the world at the behest of our employers or our spouse's employers. In my case, because of my husband's military career, we moved seventeen times in the first fourteen years of our marriage! That wasn't exactly the straight-line vision of my early dreams.

Collectively, we all lived our lives and did the best we could. We endured long hours of work, multiple jobs, and successes, disappointments, and failures alike. For those of us with children, we attended their school and sports activities whenever possible. We tried to give them everything we didn't have growing up, and more.

Along the way, many of us forgot our dreams. It wasn't that we were trying to forget. It was simply that life got in the way. In our idealistic youth, work was supposed to be the means that allowed us to create the lifestyle we had dreamed about; instead, for many of us, work became our life.

Does any of this sound familiar? If so, you are not alone. Each day I see people who have worked hard and achieved so much. And yet, despite their significant achievements, many have lost sight of their dreams. Or perhaps their dreams, wishes, and desires have changed along the way. But for the most part, they have simply forgotten what it was they were working to achieve.

My favorite saying, and one I try to live my life by, I learned from my business coach, Dan Sullivan: "Always make your future bigger than your past." This simple axiom has become my mantra. Regardless of how old you are or where you are financially, the day your past is bigger than your future is the day you start dying.

"Always make your future bigger than your past." —Dan Sullivan

---

In order to envision your future as bigger than your past, you must do an honest assessment of where you are now and where you would like to be. While it might sound laborious, this step of the Lifestyle Driven Investing process typically brings newfound energy and enthusiasm into your current life by reminding you what you are working toward. What are the details of your vision? What size is the house you want to live in? Is it the house you already own? Is it a high-rise apartment in the city, a spacious ranch, or a condo on the beach? Where and how often will you be traveling? The answers to these and other similar questions help you decide where you want to end up so you can build a plan to get you there. The lifestyle you envision is your "Preferred Future," and it basically entails being able to live your life where you want, doing what you want, and with whom you want. (To download a free Dream Sheet, go to www.thebigretirementrisk.com.)

STEP 2: QUANTIFY, QUANTIFY, QUANTIFY

Once you have reignited your dreams and have a clear picture of your Preferred Future, you're ready to deploy the numbers you came up with in chapter 5. Step 2 involves putting all four stories of the house together to construct a comprehensive House of Security/Retirement Lifestyle Sheet.

Figure 6.1 is the desired House of Security/Retirement Lifestyle Sheet for Eddie and Annie, our hypothetical couple from chapter 5. Keep in mind this is a very fluid exercise, and your personalized House of Security will obviously be unique to you. The diagram on the following page will give you a general idea.

After you have quantified your expenses, you need to quantify the other half of the equation: your expected sources of income.

STEP 3: DEFINE YOUR EXPECTED SOURCES OF INCOME

Once you have identified your Needs, Wants, Likes, and Wishes, you must figure out how you are going to pay for them. To do this

Total Annual Expenses

Needs	Annual
Personal Residence	$ 56,350
Food	$ 6,000
Clothing	$ 6,600
Medical	$ 9,200
Utilities	$ 15,000
Transportation	$ 8,400
Miscellaneous	$ 2,650
Total Needs	**$ 104,200**
Wants	
Travel	$ 12,000
Hobbies	$ 4,500
Entertainment	$ 9,000
Personal Care	$ 3,900
Other	$ 2,000
Total Wants	**$ 31,400**
Likes	
Vacation Home	
Boat	
Recreation	
Education	
Other	
Total Likes	
Wishes	
Heirs	
Charities	
Gifts to Trust	
Other	
Total Wishes	
Total Annual Expenses	**$ 135,600**

Figure 6.1: Eddie and Annie's House of Security/Retirement Lifestyle Sheet

we return to the common denominator of every Preferred Future, cash flow.

Begin by asking the following questions: What sources of income do you expect to have in retirement? Do you expect to receive a pension or Social Security? Keep in mind, little is carved in stone in our modern economy.

My husband, Bob, is a pilot for a commercial airline and has hopes of receiving his pension in retirement. For planning purposes, however, we are not counting on it. Some airlines have had their pension obligations to employees erased through bankruptcy. An advantage of our not relying on Bob's pension is that it will be a great bonus if it does come through rather than a huge disappointment if it does not. If your company does have a pension plan, you may want to do some research to determine its financial stability.

Social Security is another income source to consider, although assuming full benefits may be risky, especially if your retirement is more than ten years away. As funding and deficit problems mount, benefits could end up being reserved for the indigent or at least means-tested for individuals and households.

Any other dependable income sources you expect to have in retirement, such as rents, royalties, or even payments from a divorce or legal settlement, should also be noted. Add all of the numbers into one total expected income. Do not include expected returns on your current portfolio holdings at this stage; those holdings will be considered in Step 4.

Here are Eddie and Annie's expected income sources:

Income Sources	Monthly	Annual
Pension	$ 0	$ 0
Social Security	$ 2,400	$ 28,800
Rental Properties	$ 2,000	$ 24,000
Alimony	$ 0	$ 0
Deferred Compensation	$ 0	$ 0
Royalties	$ 400	$ 4,800
Other:	$ 0	$ 0
Total Income Sources	**$ 4,800**	**$ 57,600**

STEP 4: CALCULATE YOUR EXISTING FINANCIAL RESOURCES

In this step, list the liquid assets you would be open to converting into investments that provide income to support your lifestyle. Cash savings, stocks, bonds, and retirement accounts are common examples. Make sure you do not include the value of any assets whose income you used in Step 3.

Here are Eddie and Annie's current liquid financial resources:

Resource	Value
Cash and Equivalents	$ 20,000
Equities: stocks, equity funds, etc.	$ 1,140,000
Fixed Income: bonds, bond funds, etc.	$ 260,000
Commodities: oil and gas, precious metals, etc.	$ 0
Real Estate Investment Trusts	$ 0
Alternative Investments/Private Placements	$ 0

Retirement Plans: IRA, 401(k), 403(b), etc.	$	380,000
Other	$	0
Total Resources	**$**	**1,800,000**

STEP 5: FIND THE GAPS

Now it's time to put all the numbers together. Subtract the total amount needed to fund your desired lifestyle that you calculated in Step 2 from your anticipated income in Step 3. Make sure you are comparing apples to apples by using the annual figures in both cases. The result will indicate whether or not you have a shortfall to make up in order to be able to live your desired retirement lifestyle. If there is a shortfall, this is the target amount of income you will need to earn from your investments.

Here are Eddie and Annie's figures:

Expected annual income from Step 3	$	57,600
Annual desired lifestyle expenses from Step 2	$	(135,600)
Annual surplus/shortfall	**$**	**(78,000)**

Eddie and Annie face an annual shortfall of $78,000. For the purpose of this exercise, divide that figure by 5 percent—a conservative rate of income. That equates to $1,560,000, an approximation of how much of the couple's investable assets should be allocated to investments to support this particular lifestyle. In other words, $1,560,000 earning 5 percent annually will generate $78,000 in annual income—enough to cover their shortfall. Since Eddie and Annie have $1,800,000 in liquid assets they can use to generate income (Step 4), they should have no problem living out their Preferred Future.

How do your numbers compare? At this point you should have an estimate of how much income you will need for the lifestyle you wish to live in retirement, the dollar amount needed to fund your Preferred Future. If your expected income in retirement is greater than the lifestyle income needs you calculated in Step 2, congratulations! You may already be able to enjoy your desired standard of living without having to make any adjustments to your investment portfolio. If you do not yet have enough savings and income sources to fund that lifestyle, you have two choices: (1) take out some of the Wants and choose to live a simpler lifestyle, or (2) estimate the amount of additional savings you need to accumulate before retiring to support that lifestyle.

My hope is that the five steps of this exercise have helped you define your Preferred Future and realize there is still time to make your dreams come true. You should now be ready to start learning about the implementation of Lifestyle Driven Investing. This means finding precisely the right products necessary for you to reach and sustain your Preferred Future. In the next chapter, I explain Step 6, which is all about helping you make smart product and investment choices.

ERIN'S ESSENTIALS

- Planning for an undefined future can be both confusing and frustrating.
- With the right planning, you may be closer to financial independence than you think.
- You will need to find investments that allow you to use your existing assets to generate the additional income needed for you to reach your Preferred Lifestyle and financial independence.
- **Ask yourself:**
  - What do I want the rest of my life to look like?
  - How do I want to spend my time in retirement?
  - How much cash flow will that lifestyle require?
  - How much recurring income do I currently have?
  - What future income, such as Social Security, will be available to me?
  - How much additional income will I need to retire or obtain financial independence?

For more information and complimentary reports, go to
www.thebigretirementrisk.com.

CHAPTER 7

LIFESTYLE DRIVEN INVESTING: CHOOSING THE RIGHT INVESTMENT PRODUCTS

We have covered a lot of ground so far, and I want to be sure you understand a couple of things before we go any further. First, there is no perfect investment product. Period. If there were, I and about a million other people would have found it. But the bottom line is, we still have to make decisions about where to put our money and whom to trust.

> There is no perfect investment product. Period. If there were, I and about a million other people would have found it.

The second point I want to make is that we are ultimately responsible for our own success or failure. Unlike many other authors, I am not willing to claim this book is the only resource you will ever need on investing. If you want to be financially successful it is up to you to read up on investing, study a number of different strategies, and choose what makes sense for you. I can only say that what I am about to share with you has worked for me, personally, and has worked for hundreds of my clients. What you do with this information is up to you.

Finally, I want you to understand that I have tried to make this discussion timeless. Since I have no idea what the economic environment is like as you read this book, I am going to give you broad characteristics to help you evaluate investment options. Rather than give you a model with specific investments, I am going to give you a set of criteria against which you can evaluate all of your choices. Think of this as a checklist, something you can refer to when you visit your financial advisor or do your own research.

With these "rules of the road" established, and the five steps you completed in the previous chapter, you are ready to move on to Step 6 and categorize your investment options into three categories based on their ability to help you create and maintain your Preferred Future: Lifestyle, Hybrid, and Non-Lifestyle. After we have defined each category, we can discuss the important distinctions between each one. Once you understand the specific criteria that you need to consider before choosing an investment product, you will be much more prepared to find the financial instruments that are right for you.

LIFESTYLE INVESTMENT CRITERIA

A fundamental part of your investment philosophy should be to fund all Needs with Lifestyle investments. Go back and look at the items you specified as Needs in your House of Security. These are the items you want to be sure you can always afford. Since these are imperatives, you should have a strict set of criteria for the investments you choose for this category. For Wants and Likes, you can perhaps be less stringent, but Needs must be met.

Here is the set of criteria to use as a benchmark for product selection in the Lifestyle category:

- The investment must produce an income, either now or in the future (when you need it).
- The income this investment produces must be considered safe or predictable or guaranteed. (Note: These are broad guidelines, hence the word "or" between each attribute. Rarely will you find an investment that includes all of these attributes, but I believe the investment product you are considering should be able to defend at least one of these words.)
- Ideally, you want to place your Lifestyle dollars into some sort of legal entity that may provide a level of asset protection in the event you face a lawsuit. If you were to accidentally injure someone, you wouldn't want the dollars that support your basic needs to be available to satisfy a judgment. These provisions vary by state, and you should always get professional legal advice for any asset-protection strategy. This discussion goes far beyond the scope of this book—but some popular structures for consideration include "qualified" accounts such as IRAs, annuity/insurance products in certain states, and more complex structures such as limited partnerships and LLCs.

- If at all possible, a Lifestyle investment should have the ability to achieve some element of growth or appreciation. This is not a deal breaker, but it certainly is nice when possible.

Lifestyle investments must produce an income either now or in the future, and they must be safe or predictable or guaranteed. If at all possible, they should be protected by a legal entity and include some element of growth or appreciation.

I have intentionally made the criteria for this category very strict because what we are asking these products to do is vital. These investments must be the cash cow to fund your retirement Needs. That is an extremely important job, and one that should not be taken lightly. You can possibly afford to take risks with other dollars—dollars that will not be needed to pay your mortgage or light bill—but not until you have locked down at least the money required for your basic Needs.

No matter when you are reading this book, I assure you there are investments available that meet these stringent specifications. The point is to have and maintain criteria, rather than having no idea why you are choosing one investment vehicle over another.

Fund your Needs with
Lifestyle investments.

HYBRID INVESTMENT CRITERIA

A Hybrid investment has some, but not all, characteristics of a Lifestyle investment. For example, a Hybrid investment such as a dividend-earning stock may produce an income, but that income may not be considered safe or guaranteed.

Another type of Hybrid investment might not produce an income, but the underlying investment could be considered safe or predictable or guaranteed. For instance, some existing investment vehicles do not produce an income but have FDIC insurance on them, so they could be considered safe and/or potentially guaranteed.

Hybrid investments might produce an income, but you could not say the income was safe or predictable or guaranteed. On the other hand, Hybrid investments might not produce an income, but the underlying investment could be considered safe or predictable or guaranteed.

Many investments that are popular with retirees would be classified as a Hybrid. For example, preferred stocks, which share some characteristics of bonds and some characteristics of stocks, tend to pay high regular dividends. These are not guaranteed, of course, and if the company falls on hard times the dividend can be suspended. The same is true of dividend-paying common stocks such as public utilities.

There is nothing inherently wrong with using a Hybrid investment to produce some or all of your cash flow—you just need to know what you are getting and not getting in terms of safety, predictability, and guarantees. You might use Hybrid investments to fund Wants, Likes, or Wishes, but you should rarely, if ever, consider one of these products to fund Needs.

Fund your Wants, Likes, or Wishes with Hybrid investments.

NON-LIFESTYLE INVESTMENT CRITERIA

As you may be able to guess, the Non-Lifestyle category is for investments that meet none of the criteria of a Lifestyle investment. That is, they generally do not produce regular, predictable income, and they could not be considered safe, predictable, or guaranteed.

Non-Lifestyle investments are primarily growth opportunities and could include all of the traditional investment vehicles like stocks, bonds, mutual funds, and exchange-traded funds (ETFs), as well as many alternative investments available in the marketplace—hedge funds, commodities, foreign currencies, and hard assets such as gold, silver, or platinum.

Just like Hybrid investments, there is nothing inherently wrong with Non-Lifestyle investments; you simply need to understand the role they play. Since these investments generally do not produce an income—remember the Renoir painting I mentioned in chapter 2?—you should not plan on using them to pay for basic living expenses. Sometimes, due to the risk associated with these types of investments, they can offer the potential of higher returns. For this reason, many people use them after they have locked down their Lifestyle Needs, and they may use them to fund Likes and Wishes. For example, if they get a great windfall on a Non-Lifestyle investment, they may decide to get the boat they have always wanted.

Please note that your *ability* to take more risk is not the same as your *willingness* to do so. You may have the ability in that you have sufficient funds to take a risk without jeopardizing your lifestyle, but this does not mean you are comfortable doing so. On the other hand, you may have a high willingness to take a risk, but it would not be wise to do so if it would subject your basic lifestyle to the roller coaster commonly referred to as the stock market. Your primary objective should be to secure your Preferred Lifestyle so that you are free to pursue more risky offerings *if* you desire.

Use Non-Lifestyle investments only after you have secured your lifestyle, and then only as you are comfortable.

ACCREDITED INVESTMENTS

There is one other category of investments you might want to consider if you are legally eligible to do so. These investments are available only to investors who are defined by the Securities and Exchange Commission as "accredited investors." An accredited investor is a natural person who has at least $1 million in investable assets, excluding their personal residence.

People who fit this category have access to a stratum of investment opportunities such as hedge funds and angel investor networks that I am not allowed to discuss with people who do not meet the federally mandated definition. If you meet the specifications and would like to know more about the opportunities and risks of these private investments, I encourage you to reach out to a trusted advisor for more information.

THE EVOLUTION OF THE THREE CATEGORIES

Now that I have outlined the criteria for Lifestyle, Hybrid, and Non-Lifestyle investments, I want to discuss the philosophy behind this separation in more depth. Why do I draw such a hard line between the categories? What does the distinction between Lifestyle investments and the other two groups matter to you and your portfolio? To answer these questions I am going to share the evolution of the categories with you.

For many years, my firm focused solely on Lifestyle investments, the income-producing side of the equation. Truth be told, many of our clients chose to have both their Needs and their Wants funded with investments that met the Lifestyle investment criteria anyway. In other words, they locked down as much of their

Preferred Lifestyle as possible with investments that produced an income that was safe or predictable or guaranteed. Once our clients' lifestyles were provided for, they were free to go out and invest in every other type of investment they could conceive of, and many of them worked with other brokers and advisors to do so.

Then our clients began urging us to open a division to handle the Non-Lifestyle side of the business as well, which we did. Once we decided to open a division of our business to recommend these other types of investments, we had to really evaluate what the business would look like. We already had an amazing model in place that worked very well in providing for our clients' Lifestyle Needs and we wanted to provide the same level of service for their Non-Lifestyle investments.

To that end, we listened not only to what our clients said but also to what they did not say. During this process, we realized our clients' risk tolerances were not always what they thought they were. Even though they told us they wanted to have access to every type of investment available and were okay with taking risks with their Non-Lifestyle dollars, those statements were not always true. It confirmed for me what I already knew: investors have a lot of tolerance for risk when the financial markets are going up, and they have no tolerance for risk when the markets are going down. No need for a risk tolerance questionnaire!

As my firm obtained more and more access to investment products due to our broker-dealer affiliation, we found an increasing number of investment vehicles that shared characteristics of both the Lifestyle and Non-Lifestyle categories. Thus, the Hybrid category was born.

Now that you understand how I categorize the world of investments and the strategy used to deploy them, let's take a look at how this compares to the message being preached by Wall Street and work on determining the best strategy for your money.

MAKE YOUR MONEY WORK FOR YOU— KNOW WHY YOU OWN WHAT YOU OWN

Matching individual investments to individual retirement Needs and Wants is called "mental accounting" in behavioral finance. I call it Lifestyle Driven Investing. Wall Street would tell you not to do this and instead rely on systematic withdrawals from one big portfolio, all of which could be subjected to a 40 percent decline in the markets as we saw in 2008. This goes to show how truly out of touch much of the industry is when it comes to meeting the needs of investors—especially retirees. All investor Needs and Wants are not created equal. Food and shelter take a higher priority than do vacations and luxury cars. Shouldn't your investment plan reflect this reality?

The bottom line is this: as a new way to think about money, Lifestyle Driven Investing puts an emphasis on cash flow to support a predefined lifestyle. My basic philosophy is that you should make your money work so you don't have to. This strategy relies on having a well-defined philosophy about money and what it is supposed to do for you.

When I say "philosophy about money," I am talking about the presumed role of money in your life. All of us develop certain beliefs during our childhood, and we refine these beliefs throughout our lives. Many of us are not aware we even have a philosophy about money; fewer still can articulate theirs.

Quite often a prospective client will come into our office carrying a large binder full of investment statements from various financial institutions. Sometimes there are literally hundreds of stock, bond, mutual fund, and ETF positions. So I ask them, "Can you tell me what all of these investments are supposed to do for you?" I wait for an answer. Usually, there isn't one. Not wanting to insult them, I continue: "It looks like you rely heavily on the advice of your current advisor(s). Assuming that is the case, can you tell me your advisor's philosophy about money?" Again, silence.

I move on to my next round of questions. "What is the plan for these investments?" I ask. "Are you going to own them for a little while and then sell them and buy other investments? What happens when you retire? What happens if we have a long, sustained downturn in the financial markets? What is the plan for creating a regular and predictable cash flow to sustain your lifestyle and pay your bills?" Rarely do I get answers. I find that disturbing.

When I realize the person sitting in front of me cannot articulate his own philosophy about money, I ask my closing question. "If you don't know your philosophy about money, how can you possibly know what your money is supposed to do for you?" Again, I often receive a blank stare.

Truthfully, many people do not know their specific philosophy about money. When I first meet with them, they have often interviewed several planners and are trying to decide who would be the best fit for them. I always take this opportunity to share the Lifestyle Driven Investing philosophy. I describe the exact process I have laid out here—reigniting your dreams and designing your Preferred Future. I share with them my belief that their money is supposed to create the cash flow mechanism through which they will live out the second half of their lives.

The entire purpose of this book is to put all investment choices into perspective and to create a framework for making decisions that support what many retired clients want: to create and sustain a level of predictable cash flow that supports their lifestyles in good times and bad, up markets and down.

Some of our new clients have the urge to cling to their original portfolios and ways of thinking about money and investing. Their previous advisors and brokers are often ardent defenders of the types of investments we would only consider as part of their Non-Lifestyle investments. As a result, their portfolios are normally built using traditional investment strategies. These new clients can occasionally be skeptical of our approach, since it is vastly different from everything they have been taught. However, all it takes is an especially volatile time in the markets and many people quickly realize they need to start playing a whole new game in order to survive. Is there a reason why our clients have consistently maintained their lifestyles in the face of sustained bear markets? Absolutely. Because the Lifestyle Driven Investment philosophy works.

WHY IT WORKS

Though Lifestyle Driven Investing is very simple, it is also very powerful. I know this because I saw it work in the crash of 2008. Many other advisors had to call their clients and tell them they would likely have to reduce their lifestyle and associated expenses by 30 to 50 percent (or more) due to their underlying market values going down. What a horrible message that must have been to deliver. Worse yet, if the advisors chose not to call their clients and encourage them to reduce their lifestyles proportionate to the amount of decline in their overall portfolios, their retired clients ran the risk of simply running out of money.

Remember, many of these retirees are relying on systematic withdrawals from their portfolios to create their income. Theoretically, the "balance" between stocks and bonds is supposed to work: when one asset class goes up, the other presumably goes down, and vice versa. Unfortunately, we have seen many situations, such as during the financial crisis of 2008, where that isn't exactly how things pan out. In eighteen months, the S&P 500 plummeted nearly 1,000 points.

Ideally, you want the cash flow element of the investment to be independent of the underlying value of the asset. This is why Lifestyle investments deserve to be in a different category from the investments that fall into the Non-Lifestyle group.

This approach coincides closely with the teachings of investment guru Robert Kiyosaki. He heavily promoted the idea of cash flow as the real ticket to financial independence in his original book, *Rich Dad, Poor Dad*. Kiyosaki's point of entry was a little different than mine; he promoted the idea of buying real estate rental properties for the cash flow created by the associated rental income. While Kiyosaki was certainly an advocate of buying properties at good prices, he was not necessarily concerned about capital appreciation. His philosophy in this strategy was not to buy real estate properties in order to turn around and resell them; it was to accumulate a portfolio of income-producing properties to create cash flow to support lifestyle expenses.

I could not possibly agree more. Even during the economic

crisis, Kiyosaki's approach remained strong. It didn't matter if the perceived value of the apartment complex or other rental homes went down in value by 40 percent—as long as the rents were coming in to produce cash flow. The perceived value of the underlying building may have altered the net worth value shown on a balance sheet or financial statement, but so what? If the students of his philosophy were true to his set of rules, then they shouldn't care if their apartment complex went down by 40 percent in value . . . as long as the monthly rental income stayed stable.

The way I see it, the only difference between Kiyosaki's financial philosophy and mine is that he uses primarily real estate assets and I use "paper assets" to produce the income. The investment products we recommend are ones that individuals can easily purchase; no real estate savvy required. However, the same rules apply. It doesn't matter if the markets are down by 40 percent; as long as the monthly cash flow from our clients' investments remains stable, they should (absent unforeseen needs or circumstances) have money to pay their bills and sustain their lifestyles.

While the underlying value of the assets we use may affect the magic number that appears on your statement or balance sheet, if your assets are positioned for cash flow before anything else, then you will achieve the intended outcome with that portion of your assets. Cash flow is king.

This is not to imply that capital appreciation is not important. You simply have to prioritize what is most important: reliable cash flow, or a number on a brokerage statement that can be cut in half in the blink of an eye? I'll take cash flow any day. Not with all my money, but certainly with all the money I need to pay my everyday living expenses.

With Lifestyle Driven Investing, each investment has a specific role to play in your life. Some have a robust role to play and are superstars in terms of their income-generating capabilities. Some not only provide an income but also stock market performance with downside protection. Other investments are attractive because they offer the ability for increases in income, which could be important if our economy goes into an inflationary cycle. Some investments purposefully play lesser roles but are valuable nonetheless. The point here is that you need to know why you own what you own.

Each investment has a specific role to play in your life. Investors have been conditioned over the years to focus on saving a certain amount for retirement—their magic number, say $2 million. But this approach fails to take into account which investments are appropriate for the accumulation phase, or—arguably more important—the distribution phase. It defines money by what it is instead of by what it can do.

Now that you have a framework you can use to evaluate any investment opportunity you may find, you, too, can define your money by what it does. As I mentioned earlier, this framework should be timeless since it is not based on any specific investment. However, if you are like me, you may have already fast-forwarded in your mind and assumed that I am going to recommend that you put your money in bonds to generate cash flow. After all, traditional financial planning wisdom would say, "If you need income, buy bonds." So, in the next chapter I am going to take you through the ins and outs of bonds and show you how they may or may not be appropriate as Lifestyle investments.

ERIN'S ESSENTIALS

- There is no perfect investment. Investments themselves are neither "good" nor "bad."
- In retirement, it's all about cash flow; regular, predictable cash flow.
- In or out of retirement, you need to have an investment philosophy to help guide your decisions; use the framework of your philosophy to assist you in product selection.
- Choose to be an investment product "agnostic." View all investment options through the lens of whether or not they will serve you in achieving your lifestyle goals.
- Try to leave emotions out of the decision-making process.
- Begin evaluating investment options by classifying them into one of three categories based on the investment's ability to produce an income stream: Lifestyle (Needs), Hybrid (Wants, Likes, or Wishes), or Non-Lifestyle (growth opportunities).
- **Ask yourself:**
  - Do I know why I own the investments I currently own?
  - [If you are retired]: Do my investments, combined with other sources of recurring income, provide for my Preferred Lifestyle?
  - [If you are not yet retired]: Are my assets positioned to help me achieve financial independence with an adequate level of predictable cash flow?

For more information and complimentary reports, go to
www.thebigretirementrisk.com.

CHAPTER 8

THE SEARCH FOR RETIREMENT INCOME

In this chapter we will discuss two categories of investments that people traditionally look to as sources of retirement income: bonds and real estate. Both have advantages and disadvantages, and their use should be understood in the context of the current economic environment.

WHAT ABOUT BONDS?

Bonds are arguably one of the most popular yet most misunderstood asset classes in the marketplace. There are periods when bonds can be the absolute perfect solution for cash flow. However, this is not always the case. In fact, I would go so far as to say that buying bonds in the wrong market environment could be as dangerous as buying Florida condos in 2005.

Buying bonds in the wrong market
environment could be as dangerous
as buying Florida condos in 2005!

Before you commit a certain percentage of your portfolio to bonds, I implore you to take the time to study this chapter. I am going to describe bonds in detail, including their interesting history and how this has affected the public perception of the bond market today. Then I will discuss the many types available to help you determine what portion of your money, if any, should be invested in bonds. Knowing you will be bombarded with advice to go down this path and buy bonds, I think it is essential for you to have a good knowledge of this major asset class. Remember, my goal is for you to become a product agnostic. I want you to be able to think for yourself and not be swayed by the traditionalists who have a predetermined recipe for your retirement dollars. Their recipe may work for them but could, under certain economic circumstances, be disastrous for you.

HOW BONDS WORK

In its most basic form, a bond represents a loan an investor makes to an entity. That entity might be the U.S. government, a state, a local municipality, or a corporation. It could even be a loan to a foreign government or entity. When an entity issues bonds, they are raising capital from those who buy the bonds.

Like any other type of loan, a bond has a holding period after which the bond is said to mature as well as an interest rate associated with it (often referred to as the "coupon"). The interest rate listed on the bond is an annualized rate, and interest payments are usually made to the bondholder semiannually. For example, let's say ABC Corporation decides to raise money by issuing bonds in an attempt to grow the business, and they are offering the bonds with a 6 percent interest rate. You decide to purchase a ten-year $100,000 bond from ABC Corporation. Since 6 percent of $100,000 is $6,000, ABC Corporation would pay you $3,000 semiannually for an annual total of $6,000. At the end of the holding period—in this case, ten years—the bond matures and ABC Corporation gives you your original $100,000 back.

Let's say that five years after buying this bond, you decide you want your money back. There are still five years left before the bond matures so ABC Corporation will not pay you back yet. In order to get your money early, you would have to sell the bond on the open market. What you would be hoping for in this case is that another investor is willing to pay you $100,000 for the bond, in which case they would collect the remaining five years of interest payments and then collect the $100,000 from ABC Corporation when the bond matures. What many people do not realize is that the bond market is an actively traded market, every bit as busy and sometimes every bit as volatile as the stock market. This will become very important when we talk about interest rates a little later in the chapter.

As with any investment, there are a number of risks associated with bonds, two of which I will discuss here. The first risk has to do with the entity issuing the bonds. If that entity were to default on their interest payments or go bankrupt, you could lose some or all of your investment. To help investors evaluate the issuer risk associated with the various bonds in the marketplace, a few rating agencies exist to rank the creditworthiness of the issuers. As you can imagine, bond issuers work very hard to have a high credit rating because that makes their bonds more attractive to investors. Additionally, the higher the credit rating of the issuer, typically the lower the interest rate they are able to pay to investors on their bonds; lower risk means lower returns.

Interestingly enough, during the 2008 financial crisis, it was deemed that many of the credit rating agencies were complicit in giving ratings that in no way reflected the risk reflective of the underlying portfolios. Some investors who thought they had purchased highly rated bonds were shocked at their outcomes. I am hopeful the rating agencies have cleaned up their acts since that time, but one can never be 100 percent certain; hence, diversification among issuers is incredibly important with bonds.

The second risk associated with bonds is a potential loss in value due to a change in the interest-rate environment. When an entity issues bonds, the interest rate offered is based largely on two factors: (1) on the creditworthiness of the issuer and (2) on the prevailing interest rate in the market as a whole at the time of issue. To illustrate how changing interest rates can affect the market value of a bond, let's go back to our example of the $100,000 bond with a 6 percent interest rate.

Let's assume, from the time you purchased the bond yielding 6 percent, interest rates started to climb. In fact, for the purpose of making a point, let us say interest rates climbed very high very quickly. A year later, the prevailing rate was 10 percent for a ten-year bond from the same type of company as your bond. That is a significant increase! A brand-new investor could go out into the marketplace and command 10 percent interest for lending money. How does your 6 percent interest look in that environment? Not so good, right?

Now, recall our discussion about selling a bond before it matures. If someone could get 10 percent on a brand-new bond of equal quality, do you think they would be willing to pay you the full $100,000 for your bond that is only earning 6 percent? Of course not.

This is where owning bonds can become problematic. If for any reason you need or want to sell your bond before it matures and the prevailing interest rate is higher than the rate your bond is paying, you will likely have to put your bond "on sale" in order to get rid of it. While you would likely still be able to sell your bond on the open market, you would probably have to "discount" it by a tremendous amount to do so. Thus, if interest rates climb from the time you buy your bond—all other factors being equal—the underlying value of your existing bond will likely go down.

> If interest rates climb from the time you buy your bond—all other factors being equal—the underlying value of your existing bond will likely go down.

However, the opposite is also true. Let's reverse the situation and think about what would happen if interest rates went *down* dramatically from the time you purchased a bond. In fact, let's assume the prevailing rate of return on bonds from companies similar to yours is only 2 percent. Suddenly, your 6 percent interest rate looks very attractive in the marketplace, doesn't it? In this case, you are probably going to be able to make a profit if you sell your bond, what is referred to as selling at a premium. If interest rates decline from the time you own your bond—all other things being equal—the value of your existing bond will likely go up.

> ## If interest rates decline from the time you own your bond—all other things being equal—the value of your existing bond will likely go up.

When buyers bid up the price of your 6 percent bond, the effective rate they will enjoy falls to 2 percent, the prevailing market rate. Hopefully they realize that when the bond matures, they will receive only the original face value, $100,000.

The following simple diagram best illustrates the economic principle behind bonds:

Figure 8.1

Reader: Stop!

I want to interrupt your thoughts at this juncture to have you answer one very important question. As you are reading this book or making decisions about where to put your money, what do you see in the current interest-rate environment? Are interest rates relatively low or are they relatively high? Are interest rates likely to go up or down from here?

It is critically important to have a general sense of the interest-rate environment, especially when you are deciding whether or not to buy bonds. As you are reading this book, are interest rates relatively low and expected to go up? If so, it stands to reason that if you invest in bonds now, you could expect to lose value in your underlying principal value if you end up selling your bonds prior to maturity. In a rising interest-rate environment, bond investors potentially face not only losing principal value in the bonds they currently own; they are also stuck with the lower rate instead of receiving the higher interest payments offered in the new interest-rate environment. Talk about a double whammy! An environment where interest rates are low but expected to climb is one of the most difficult and tenuous environments for bond investors.

On the other hand, as you are reading this book, interest rates may be relatively high and expected to decline. This is a bondholder's dream scenario. Every time interest rates go lower, all other things being equal, the value of bonds goes higher. People looking for income want the highest income they can get. People who own bonds in this scenario can often realize a profit on their bonds (if they sell) because income investors will pay them a premium to have access to the higher interest payments.

The truth about bonds is simple: under the *right* circumstances, they can be a valuable investment tool. In an environment where interest rates are high but declining, a bond could be one of the best investments you ever make. When interest rates are low and potentially going up, bonds can be a very poor investment choice. In that environment, bondholders should expect to see the market value of their bonds drop and be prepared for the disappointment of having their money tied up in lower-yielding bonds.

MY HISTORY WITH BONDS

My knowledge of bonds has increased dramatically over the last two decades. Anyone reading this book is likely old enough to remember the 1980s. At the time, I was an escrow officer involved in closing loans for people buying homes. Between 1981 and 1984, I was working in North Carolina, closing loans where people were paying 16 percent interest or more on their home mortgages. Sounds ludicrous, doesn't it? But the interest-rate environment back in those days had gotten out of whack. Though it is not entirely accurate, many people remember those days as the "Jimmy Carter days," with double-digit interest rates and double-digit inflation. It was a difficult time in our economy. It's hard to imagine very many people being able to afford to buy a home with mortgage interest rates at 15, 16, and 18 percent. Yet I closed a lot of loans in those days. People had gotten used to higher rates and it simply became the new norm.

In the investment world, bond returns were quickly becoming a welcome alternative to the stock market, which was just coming out of what was then one of its worst periods in recent history. The Dow Jones Industrial Average ended 1981 below its level of 1966—fifteen years without any appreciation in investors' portfolios. One of the worst bear markets in U.S. history occurred from 1973–74, when the market lost nearly half its value. It was such a long period of decline that people had pretty much given up all hope of a stock market recovery.

Since so many people at the time had been burned badly in the stock market, there weren't many "takers" willing to invest in stocks. Instead, people went to the safety of their local banks and bought certificates of deposit (CDs) and bonds, especially for their retirement income. Keep in mind, interest rates were so high in the early 1980s that even bank-guaranteed CDs were often paying higher than 20 percent. The investors who bought bonds and other fixed income securities essentially locked in those high rates.

Following those years, several policy shifts ensued, resulting in two things: First, the stock markets finally started rising again. Second, interest rates finally started falling. In fact, the next several years saw a time of steadily declining interest rates and declining inflation. Investors who owned bonds and had locked in high interest rates from the early 1980s were watching their bonds continue to rise in value. (Remember—as interest rates fall, bond values go up.) Every time they turned around, the value of their bonds went up! It was wonderful—or so they thought.

On the one hand, they liked seeing the values on their existing bonds go up. But truthfully, these higher values were a moot point unless they were prepared to sell their bonds. If they held these higher-paying bonds until maturity, they would just receive the face value of the bond. If they sold their bonds, even at a profit, the next dilemma was redeploying their cash into other income-producing investments in the overall lower interest-rate environment. It was a double-edged sword.

As many of those high-interest-paying bonds matured or got called away due to prepayment privileges held by the issuers, people on fixed incomes bemoaned the fact they had to reinvest at lower rates. They had become very accustomed to living on 15 to 20 percent interest payments on their bonds and CDs. When their CDs or bonds matured, the replacements were paying significantly lower rates of interest than before. It was quite an interesting time. Retired people longed for higher interest rates, forgetting the high inflation that went along with that time in history.

It didn't take long to notice that retirees were being forced to change their lifestyles dramatically because their calculations of what they would be able to live on in retirement were now badly flawed. Some retirees had retired assuming they would always be able to get a yield of at least 12 to 14 percent on their money. I know that sounds ludicrous now, but that had become the norm, and they based all of their lifestyle calculations on being able to get this kind of interest on their money. This goes back to the recency bias we talked about in chapter 3; we tend to put undue importance on recent events, often drawing the wrong conclusions.

Unfortunately, it became evident that many of these people either overspent because the money had been rolling in, or they shouldn't have retired in the first place. Fortunately, the saving grace for many of these retirees was that they worked in the age where companies provided retiree pensions; thus, many of them were effectively saved from financial ruin because they had pensions as well as health care benefits.

Bond investors who were not retirees but merely investors looking for capital appreciation loved the years of declining interest-rates. Many had the opportunity to sell their higher-interest-paying bonds at huge profits, and bond trading became very popular. Even I got in the game in the early 1990s, trading government zero-coupon bonds. It was fun and hugely successful. And then came 1994, when all of the above began to change.

Alan Greenspan was the chairman of the Federal Reserve, and in 1994 alone, the Federal Reserve raised interest rates six times. Multiple interest-rate hikes were unprecedented at the time and a game-changer for a lot of people. Every time interest rates went up that year, the underlying principal value of the individual bonds that people already owned went down. Retirees watched the bond values on their statements go down time after time after time that year. By the end of 1994, the value of the thirty-year treasury was down over 30 percent. In effect, the bond party that had lasted more than a decade was over.

The bond bust of 1994 was a shock to the financial markets and certainly to retirees who had gotten used to the idea that bonds were safe. Afterward, it became necessary to redefine the word "safe." For those who had continued to buy or own individual bonds, assuming the entities were still viable and still paying their interest, who could argue their money was not safe? As long as the interest payments were coming in and the client intended to hold the bond until it matured, the current value of the bonds didn't make any difference to them. It's like owning a house. Nobody goes out and gets appraisals and/or comps on their personal residence every day, because they have no need to know what their house is worth on a daily basis. It doesn't matter because the value has no relevance to them until they are actually ready to sell it.

The problem was that many retirees and those living on fixed incomes had been convinced to forgo buying individual bonds. Instead, they started investing in bond mutual funds and unit investment trusts. The problem with this new strategy was that they no longer held ownership of individual bonds with their own interest-rate and maturity date.

As we saw in our earlier example, when you own an individual bond, if you hold the bond to maturity and there is no default by the entity, you should be able to expect to receive your original principal back. In a bond mutual fund, however, an investor owns a tiny fractional piece of a large portfolio of bonds. There was no way to tell these retirees they would definitely receive all of their principal back over any period of time. In essence, they were at the mercy of three forces: the manager who managed the portfolio, the interest rate environment, and the other investors' behaviors.

In a rising-interest-rate environment, it would be very difficult for the manager of the portfolio to do anything to offset the effects higher interest rates would have on an existing pool of bonds. Even if the manager was able to buy new bonds at higher interest rates, it often wasn't enough to offset the impact. So many bond funds and other pools of bonds went down in value—and it wasn't a minor loss.

I remember a day in the summer of 1994 when a woman called me out of the blue and asked: "Erin, in January of this year, I put $1 million of my money in a Ginnie Mae fund. Now my statement says it's only worth about $800,000. Will I ever get my money back?"

Remember, in that year with six interest-rate hikes, the underlying value of any existing bond declined in value. Had the woman put her money in an individual-issue U.S. Treasury bond, I could have given her the assurance that as long as she held that bond to its full maturity, she could expect to receive her full $1 million back. But, because she had succumbed to the new wave of investing in pooled funds that held hundreds of bond certificates, there was no way to tell what she would receive back. It truly depended on what happened to the interest-rate environment. If interest rates continued to go up, it was likely her principal value would continue to go down.

Now that you have a better understanding of the history of bonds and how they work, I want to introduce you to the many different types of bonds available. The bond universe is enormous, and new forms of bond products come to the market constantly. To help you understand all the options available to you, I will describe some of the more common bonds that investors are likely to purchase.

It is important to remember that not all bonds are true Lifestyle investments. Only bonds with income that is *safe* or *predictable* or *guaranteed* can meet that distinction. Always use your own discretion when deciding which bonds or securities are right for you.

CORPORATE BONDS

Corporate bonds are the most straightforward type of bond and subsequently the easiest to understand. Very basically, they are IOUs issued by a major corporation. The credit rating of the corporation is an important factor to consider when investing in corporate bonds. Just ask investors who owned General Motors or Lehman Brothers bonds in 2008. What's the lesson to be learned? Though many people associate bonds with safety, this is clearly not always the case.

One strategy is to "ladder" your corporate bond portfolio. To create this setup, you purchase bonds with varying terms and maturity dates—say, five years, ten years, and fifteen years. As the bonds mature, you reinvest the proceeds in the longest-term bond of your ladder—fifteen-year bonds in our example. This allows investors to receive ongoing interest payments, and every five years they will receive the principal to then deploy back into the strategy. By holding the bonds until maturity, interest-rate risk is not an issue.

One of our clients, whom I will call "Chuck," had approximately $3 million to invest, all of it in an IRA. What he chose to do was to select investment-grade bonds (bonds with a rating of BBB or better) in increments of $15,000. Chuck's average yield on the portfolio was roughly 5 percent, so he could effectively count on about $150,000/year in income from his portfolio.

Chuck knew his biggest risk was that if interest rates went higher, the value of his bonds could go lower, but he was willing to accept that. He did not intend to sell any of the bonds prior to maturity, and the average of the bonds matured in eight to ten years. He figured he would have the cash again sometime in the future to redeploy the money into higher-yielding bonds if that was where interest rates were at the time. Chuck was also well aware of the risk of default by the underlying corporations. But he felt that having small positions, each representing a fractional percentage of his overall portfolio, mitigated this risk.

This was not the only money Chuck had, but this strategy effectively provided for his monthly income, along with his Social Security and some royalties from an oil well owned by his wife. Because his income was defined and relatively predictable, he was then able to be more aggressive with his Non-Lifestyle dollars. He did not favor putting many, if any, of his investment dollars in the stock market, but instead chose to invest his Non-Lifestyle dollars in private equity offerings. Today Chuck and his wife have a very comfortable lifestyle, and his strategy has worked out very happily for everyone involved.

U.S. GOVERNMENT BONDS

The U.S. government issues a variety of bonds to fund its expenditures on various programs until taxpayer revenue comes in. These bonds are deemed credit-risk-free since they are backed by the full faith and credit of the U.S. government. This certainly meets the distinction of safe, predictable, *and* guaranteed. These securities also have unique tax characteristics not enjoyed by their corporate brethren; interest income is taxable for federal income tax purposes but tax-free for state income taxes.

The most common U.S. government bond is known as a Treasury bill. The Treasury bill, or T-bill, has a life span from issuance to maturity of less than one year. Most common is the three-month T-bill. These securities are issued at a discount and pay the principal and interest at maturity. You could argue that this is not true "income" per se, but given the short time horizons involved, it is reasonable to include T-bills in the Lifestyle investment section.

The next is a Treasury note, or T-note, which has a life span of one to ten years. These bonds provide a semiannual coupon payment of interest and mature at their original value, or at par ($1,000 per bond owned).

The longer-term U.S. Treasuries are known as Treasury bonds, or T-bonds, with a life span of greater than ten years. Like T-notes, T-bonds provide semiannual coupon payments and mature at par.

As a rule, U.S. government securities are normally more affected by the movement of interest rates than other bonds are. Unlike a corporate bond, which we discussed previously, the quality rating does not impact value. That brings us back to our initial premise: if you decide to invest $10,000 or $100,000 or $1 million in U.S. government bonds and the current interest-rate environment is very low, an increase in interest rates will cause a decrease in the principal value if you have to sell prior to maturity. The amount of fluctuation that will occur depends on the magnitude of the interest-rate change and the bond's time to maturity.

For instance, the investor holding a thirty-year bond will have to wait a full thirty years for the government to pay back the bond's par (original) value. As such, the value will typically shift more than a T-bill that matures in thirty days. Theoretically, one can anticipate where interest rates might be in nine months to a year from now; however, no one has any way of knowing where interest rates will be in thirty years. Very often, the further out the maturity date of the bond, the more fluctuation there will be in its underlying value due to changes in interest rates.

TREASURY INFLATION PROTECTED SECURITIES (TIPS)

The U.S. Treasury issues inflation-indexed bonds for the same reasons they issue T-bills, T-notes, and T-bonds: as a way of raising money to fund the U.S. government's operations. Investors at home and abroad invest in TIPS because these bonds offer the unique benefit of a real fixed income.

The return you receive from a mutual fund, stock, or bond is always reported to you as a nominal amount, which means that it does not take into account the rate of inflation on your overall return. For example, if you earned 8 percent nominal and inflation was 3 percent, you really only earned about 5 percent in inflation-adjusted terms. TIPS provide an adjustment so that your interest income keeps pace with inflation. The bond's principal amount is adjusted based on the reported consumer price inflation rate. Your coupon interest payment is then based off the new "adjusted" par value for the bond. This may sound overly complicated, but the important takeaway is that TIPS, unlike regular bonds, are designed to keep pace with inflation so that your income does not lose purchasing power over time.

One negative for TIPS is they tend to be somewhat inefficient for tax purposes. The inflation adjustment is considered income, making TIPS highly inefficient in taxable accounts. It is sometimes better to hold these in an IRA or 401(k) when possible.

TIPS are potentially one of the best ways to hedge at least a portion of your investment portfolio against inflation. Like other bonds, the value of TIPS fluctuates with changes in the underlying interest rates. But unlike other bonds, TIPS provide some protection from increasing interest rates, since rising interest rates tend to correlate with rising inflation.

As of early October 2010, the interest rate for five-year TIPS was at 0.5 percent. At this rate, you would need $20 million to generate an annual income of $100,000. Hopefully at the time you're reading this, other alternatives are available that can provide the required income with less capital involved.

MUNICIPAL BONDS

Like the federal government, state and local governments have to raise funds for operations too. These local governments issue what are known as municipal bonds, or munis. Municipal bonds are often referred to as tax-free bonds since the interest generated is free from federal income tax and often from state income tax. For some higher-income investors, municipal bond interest can be taxable under the "Alternative Minimum Tax." This is something you clearly want to avoid, so make sure that your tax advisor has a good handle on the tax laws in your municipality.

Munis are rated by the major rating agencies based on the credit quality of the issuer introducing credit risk. Due to this risk, several insurance companies, such as the Municipal Bond Insurance Association Corporation and the American Municipal Bond Assurance Corporation, provide credit risk insurance to ensure that the interest and principal are paid to investors.

To make a return comparison between a taxable bond and a muni bond you must determine the muni bond's taxable equivalent yield (TEY). This is done by dividing the yield of the muni bond by 1 minus your highest marginal tax bracket. For example, let's assume you are in the 35 percent tax bracket. Muni bond A is currently yielding 3.5 percent and the corporate bond is yielding 5 percent. At first glance, it seems like a no-brainer to go with the corporate bond. But we are not comparing apples to apples. To make the comparison, we must calculate the TEY as 3.5 percent / (1 - 35%) = 5.38 percent. In this example, you would actually be better off investing in the 3.5 percent tax-free bond because it provides a higher after-tax return than does the corporate bond paying 5 percent. (Note: there may be instances when Alternative Minimum Tax applies, so always consult your tax advisor.)

Municipal bonds are distinguished as either general obligation (GO) or revenue (rev) bonds. State, city, or local governments issue GOs for general purposes. Interest and principal payments on these bonds are backed by the full faith and credit of the issuing municipality. In other words, local tax revenues generated from sales tax, property taxes, and local income taxes are used to make good on these bonds.

Rev bonds are issued for special projects, like hospitals or toll roads. When a city wants to raise money to fund a specific project, it will issue bonds for the specific purpose of building the hospital or the toll road. Bond interest and principal is repaid through the revenue created by the underlying project. The taxpayers of the municipality are not responsible for funding the bonds. There are many different types of rev bonds, but they all basically function the same way, with a specific amount of the operating profit from the funded project paying the interest to bondholders.

Until the financial crisis of 2008, general obligation bonds were normally considered safer than revenue bonds because they are backed by the full faith and credit of the particular state, city, or municipality issuing the bond. Theoretically, the state, city, or local government could raise property taxes, sales taxes, or income taxes to cover bond interest (the majority of these tax increases must be voted on by the citizenry). But in the wake of the recession, some people are leery and somewhat fearful of general obligation bonds. They fear that the current shortfalls in state and local income may mean difficult days ahead when it comes time for municipalities to make good on bond interest payments—that the tax revenues just won't be there.

Regardless of the perceived risks, many people like municipal bonds because they provide federally tax-free interest income and, depending on the state, the interest income might be free from state income taxes as well. In addition, those who are nervous about a municipality failing to meet its obligations might want to purchase insured bonds. However, for many companies during the '08–'09 market upheaval, it turned out that insurers did not all have the requisite reserves to make good on their promises.

Just as you should be concerned about the health of the underlying company if you were investing in a corporate bond, you want to carefully review the health of the underlying municipalities. The economic crisis of 2008 was a perfect storm for Pennsylvania and many other states. Not only did property values go down; people defaulted on their mortgage loans in large numbers as well.

Many people pay their property taxes with their mortgage payment via escrow. It follows that if residents were not going to pay their mortgage payments, they would not be particularly likely to pay their property taxes either. Add that to the evaporation of jobs, which affected state income tax and sales tax revenues, and you have serious trouble. This clearly put a strain on the budgets of California and other states hit hard by the housing crisis, inevitably affecting their ability to make good on bond interest payments.

The biggest problem, however—the elephant in the room that no one wants to mention—is the state of public pensions. Here, the numbers get staggering. As of this writing, states have less than 75 percent of the funds they need to adequately cover their workers' retirements. The Pew Institute estimates that the shortfall is over a trillion dollars. Yes, that is trillion, with a *t*. Just to give you an example of how exponentially larger a trillion is than a million or a billion, here is an illustration: a million seconds is 11.5 days, a billion seconds is 31.71 years, and a trillion seconds is just over 31,688 years!

The point of this discussion is to make you clearly aware that municipal bonds, which have been the favored income investment for wealthy retirees, may not be the slam dunk they once were. Munis might still have a place in your portfolio, but make sure that you understand the risks involved. Also, be sure to never concentrate too much of your portfolio in any one state's or locality's bonds. You do not want your vital Lifestyle dollars put at risk.

SUMMARY: WHEN TO USE BONDS TO CREATE INCOME

After reading this chapter, you should have a better understanding of bonds, how they work, and what drives their yield and underlying value. Depending upon the interest-rate environment at the time you are reading this book, bonds could certainly be a viable income source. I used them extensively for retirement income in the 1990s when interest rates were high and stable or coming down. As of this writing, interest rates are at historical lows, so buying bonds now is not as attractive as it once was. That doesn't mean you shouldn't use them; you just need to be aware of the risks. I would caution you on one point: If the interest-rate environment is low, yet you still want to own bonds, be sure you are buying only the individual issues (not funds or exchange-traded funds) and create ladders with multiple issuers that mature over various time periods. Like Chuck, the client we discussed in this chapter, you want your bond exposure spread out in small increments so you know the limit of your exposure to each situation and to the prevailing interest-rate environment as a whole.

THE SEARCH FOR INCOME: WHAT ABOUT REAL ESTATE?

Owning income-producing real estate has been a viable and successful method for creating retirement income for as long as our country has been in existence. It has always been known that millions of people need a place to live, a place to work, a place to shop, and often a place to store their extra "stuff." Thus, being a landlord of residential, commercial, office, retail, and self-storage real estate has proven to be extremely successful for those who have chosen the path of income-producing real estate. That being said, many of the people with whom we work have had successful careers as corporate executives or business owners and have not had the luxury of time to focus on creating a portfolio of income-producing properties that would spin off income to fund their retirement lifestyle needs. The good news is that in today's world numerous professionals have identified, purchased, and now manage portfolios of income-producing real estate that we can tap into. The following section will discuss the pros and cons of investing in Real Estate Investment Trusts (REITs). Although there are many different types of REITs, they generally fall under two broad categories: Non-Listed/Non-Traded REITs and Publicly Traded REITs. In practice, I often use the first category, Non-Listed/Non-Traded REITs, for retirement income and usually place them in either the Lifestyle category or the Hybrid category, depending upon the issuer, track record, and current economic environment. I do not use Publicly Traded REITs as Lifestyle or Hybrid investments because they trade like a stock on the major stock exchanges and can have periods of extreme volatility in the share price. I would only consider investing in a Publicly Traded REIT with Non-Lifestyle investment dollars.

A GENERAL OVERVIEW OF REITS

A REIT is a pooled investment like a mutual fund. Instead of holding stocks or bonds, however, a REIT purchases and manages real estate assets. These assets can include capital appreciation opportunities, income-generating opportunities, or the purchase of mortgages and other debt associated with real estate.

REITs are provided special tax treatment if they meet certain requirements. By law, a REIT must invest at least 75 percent of its assets in real estate, derive at least 75 percent of gross income from rents and mortgage interest, and—the big one—distribute at least 90 percent of net investment income to shareholders. The typical corporation will not pay out 90 percent of earnings for a multitude of reasons, making them less advantageous for those seeking income from their investments. REITs, on the other hand, pay out dividends that typically range from 2 to 8 percent of your investment each year.

I have not always been a fan of REITs and still shy away from Publicly Traded REITs, as they certainly do not meet the criteria of Lifestyle investments. Publicly Traded REITs are purchased and traded among investors on the stock market during normal trading hours. This means their value fluctuates on the whims and emotions of market participants rather than on the intrinsic value of the underlying properties or cash flow.

The lesser-known type of REIT is a Non-Listed/Non-Traded REIT. The benefit with this type of investment is that it effectively cancels out the "noise" of the trading floor. These REITs are revalued regularly (typically annually), and the price is adjusted based on an expert's valuation of the underlying assets, along with the value of the cash flow being generated by the REIT. For this reason, the underlying value of Non-Traded/Non-Listed REITs tends to be more stable on a day-to-day basis.

Like every investment, REITs have their pros and cons. A few of the negative aspects of REITs are that the dividends are taxed as ordinary income, which could be a concern if you are in a high tax bracket. This issue can be avoided, of course, by simply buying a REIT inside an IRA account, which is what many of my clients do. Another downside is a potential lack of liquidity depending on the buy-back provisions of the issuing company and due to a more sparsely traded over-the-counter market.

Another potential downside to private or Non-Listed REITs is, since they are not publicly traded, they are not required to file the same paperwork, financial statements, and reports with the Securities and Exchange Commission and other regulatory bodies that oversee the public markets. As a result, there is less transparency with these investments than with those that are publicly traded. If you are interested in this type of REIT, you need to find a broker or advisor who is willing to do her own due diligence to determine the viability and reliability of the management company.

Should anyone consider a Non-Traded REIT for lifestyle income? To answer that question, let's first take a look at the demographics. The information from *Grubb & Ellis 2010* in Figure 8.2 shows the breakdown between seniors and baby boomers and the primary issues of concern for each group.

This annual report by Grubb & Ellis reveals that health care is the common concern of these two generations. Hence, REITs that invest in hospitals, nursing homes, outpatient facilities, and other health care facilities might be viable for investment consideration. In addition, it appears that both generations will be downsizing from their McMansions and moving to smaller homes and/or multifamily housing, in addition to assisted-living facilities. REIT investments that address this demographic migration might also be worthy of consideration. The common wisdom has been to stay ahead of the needs of the baby boom generation, as they have always had (and continue to have) a huge influence on all major markets.

Seniors	Baby Boomers
Elders of the Boomers	Children of the Greatest Generation
Age 65+	Born between 1946 and 1964
34 million in size	77 million in size
12 percent of the population	27 percent of the population
Issues relevant to them:	
• Health care	• Health care
• Travel	• Financial services
• Senior housing	• Empty nest housing
• Leisure activities	• Convenient shopping
• Transportation	• Dining out

Figure 8.2: Grubb & Ellis 2010

Just keep in mind, some REITs produce income that is predictable enough to fall into the category of Lifestyle investments, but certainly not any could be considered safe or guaranteed.

I hope this chapter has been helpful in differentiating between various types of bonds, securities, and similar investment options, outlining the pros and cons of the many different varieties. Now I want to turn our attention to a less traditional and potentially lesser-known method of generating retirement income. What follows is a candid look at annuities and the role they can play in an investment portfolio.

ERIN'S ESSENTIALS

- Having a general understanding of the interest-rate environment when you invest in bonds is critical because owning bonds in a rising interest-rate environment can be disastrous to your overall plan.
    - If interest rates go up, the value of an existing bond will likely go down.
    - If interest rates go down, the value of an existing bond will likely go up.
- While some bonds may offer a degree of safety over certain other investments, bonds as a whole are far from a risk-free investment.
- The risks associated with bonds include default risk, reinvestment risk, and interest-rate risk.
- Although bonds can be an appropriate investment under the *right* circumstances, they need to be evaluated just like anything else and should *not* always be considered "safe."
- **Ask yourself:**
    - Where are interest rates right now?
    - Are they generally high or low?
    - Are rates expected to rise or fall from here?

For more information and complimentary reports, go to
www.thebigretirementrisk.com.

CHAPTER 9

THE SEARCH FOR INCOME CONTINUES: WHAT ABOUT ANNUITIES?

M ost people have heard the word "annuity" in some context, but there doesn't really seem to be a good working knowledge of the different types of annuities that exist today paired with enough unbiased information to help people determine whether or not an annuity makes sense for them. Oftentimes, people have heard one side of the story, either for or against annuities, but what they don't realize is the built-in biases that exist, depending on where the information is coming from. With that in mind, your job as a product agnostic is to learn to evaluate the pros and cons of every type of investment for yourself and become the informed decision maker you were meant to be.

To put our annuity discussion in the context of this book, remember that Lifestyle investments must provide an income, either now or in the future, and the income should be safe or predictable or guaranteed. Annuities fall into this category. In fact, other than U.S. government issues, insurance company products are the only investments where the word "guaranteed" can legally be used. The biggest difference in the use of the word "guaranteed" here is that the U.S. government's promise is based on its taxing ability, whereas a guarantee by an insurance company is based on the claims-paying ability of the underlying company.

However, as a result of the failures of several insurance companies in the 1970s and 1980s, today's insurance companies are subject to strict regulations at the state level and are required to have adequate capital to meet their liabilities to investors.

> Other than U.S. government issues, insurance company products are the only investments where the word "guaranteed" can legally be used.

Interestingly enough, over the past twenty-five years, Wall Street and many financial advisors have vehemently discounted annuities as a viable alternative. But since the 2008 market meltdown, we have seen a significant shift in their attitudes toward annuities, with more and more stockbrokers and financial advisors recommending them for their clients. For those who have not changed their attitudes, it may be worth taking a deeper look at their motives. Wall Street has a tendency to belittle and/or discount any investment offering they do not manufacture. Why would they support any investment that benefits their competition and ultimately takes money out of their own coffers?

When I see Wall Street or the mainstream media vigorously deride something, I pay attention and do my homework. If the investment looks good and passes the "smell test," I go back to my primary criteria to see if the investment works and if it is a good fit for my clients. What I have learned with overwhelming consistency is that investors in or near retirement have one primary concern: they want to make sure that their current lifestyle is protected. That's it. They want to be able to spend time doing what they want to do—things like travel, leisure activities, and spending time with family and friends. They do not want to be worried about their money or their income. When thought about from that perspective, annuities are certainly worth considering.

In this chapter, we will take a good look at annuities. I want to help you understand the different kinds of annuities that exist, how they compare to each other, and how they compare to the rest of the investment products out there. I will also share with you what other experts have to say about annuities and will position them in our current economic environment to help you make an informed decision about whether or not these are right for you.

THE LANGUAGE OF ANNUITIES

There are many types of annuities in the marketplace, and correspondingly, there is a lot of confusion about which kinds, if any, are appropriate to use as Lifestyle investments. One big problem is the lack of terms to adequately explain how different types of annuities work. The result is that people tend to lump all annuities into the same pool and, with limited knowledge, deem them as collectively good or bad.

I like some annuities and don't like others, but I make that determination on a case-by-case basis. I also keep an open mind as I see various product offerings come and go. Just as in any other industry, investment products are consumer-driven, and we have certainly seen interesting annuity products come and go over the last decade. Keep in mind, the fact that they are one of the few asset classes that can use the word "guaranteed" is probably reason enough to want to have a better understanding of them so you can rule them either in or out of your portfolio.

Annuities seem to have a language of their own, which adds to the confusion surrounding this type of investment. In order to have a discussion about annuities, it is important for us to be on the same page as far as terminology is concerned. Following is a list of terms that will help get our discussion started.

Terminology Bank

Annuity: In its most basic form, an annuity is a type of investment that guarantees monthly payments for the rest of a person's life. This is very similar to the concept of a pension except that an insurance company, rather than someone's employer, is responsible for the payments. For this reason, annuities are sometimes thought of as self-funded pensions.

Annuitant: Since an annuity guarantees payments for the duration of a person's life, the annuitant is the person whose life the payments are based on. Whereas life insurance pays a death benefit when the insured person dies, an annuity makes payments for as long as the annuitant lives. Life insurance is used to mitigate the risk of someone dying prematurely and covers the expenses or loss of income associated with their death. An annuity contract mitigates the risk of someone living longer than expected and running out of money before they die. Sound familiar?

Premiums: There are two ways of "funding" an annuity contract: pay all at once, known as a single premium, or pay over time. Whether you pay in a lump sum or over time, you can elect to delay receiving income or you can begin receiving income immediately. If you delay receiving income, the policy is known as a deferred annuity; if you begin taking income immediately, it is an immediate annuity. If you are looking at a single-premium immediate annuity, you should know exactly what that means. This type of policy requires a lump sum payment that is immediately "annuitized." If you are looking at a deferred annuity, you know that the policy is paid for over time and may or may not be annuitized at some point in the future, depending on your choice. With deferred annuities, you generally have the ability to review your income options at the time you are ready to begin an income stream.

Fixed annuities: Some annuities provide for a payment structure similar to a certificate of deposit from a bank. In these contracts, the insurance company pays monthly income payments for a defined period of time (say five years) and then returns the balance of the investment to the contract holder. These contracts would not be considered "annuitized."

Traditional annuitization: This is the term used to describe the reception of the monthly payments from an annuity contract. In other words, when you annuitize a sum of money, you give it to an insurance company in the form of a premium payment in exchange for a pre-defined stream of income for the rest of your life. Note: not all insurance contracts must be "annuitized" in order for you to receive income.

Pros and Cons of Annuitization

If you elect to annuitize a contract, there are many variations and choices when it comes to annuitizing a sum of money. For example, you can elect to have payments made over one person's lifetime or you can elect a "joint and last survivor" option that pays out over the lifetimes of two people. You may also have the option of electing a period certain, which means you will get an income stream for the rest of your life or for a defined period of time, whichever is longer. For instance, if you purchased an immediate annuity with a ten-year period certain, you would receive an income stream for the rest of your life. However, if you died two years into the contract, your beneficiaries would receive the remaining eight years of payments.

One downside to annuitization—and the reason we use this form of income creation sparingly—is that it generally does not allow the owner to leave a death benefit to his or her heirs. Effectively, in consideration of the insurance company agreeing to pay the annuitant a guaranteed income stream for the rest of his or her life, the trade-off is that the insurance company gets to keep the premium money after the annuitant dies, regardless of the amount of payouts that were made. In the case of a period-certain contract, there may be some remuneration to the heirs for a certain number of missed payments, but generally speaking this form of annuity contract is a "bet" with the insurance company; the bet is on the annuitant's longevity. If the person on whose life it is based lives longer than average life expectancy, the investor wins by having an income stream for his or her entire life. If, however, the person dies prior to life expectancy, the math works out in favor of the insurance company.

Even with this in mind, annuitizing an income stream may provide the single greatest source of guaranteed income so it is definitely a viable option in the right situation. This could easily be justified for people who either have no children or have set aside other assets to leave their children. Perhaps they have already purchased life insurance for that purpose. We have also seen plenty of people who do not feel any obligation to leave an inheritance to anyone, in which case the lack of death benefit is not a concern.

WHAT ECONOMISTS SAY

Interestingly enough, in contrast to the Wall Street position that often derides the use of annuities in any way, shape, or form, the Wharton School of Business has conducted significant studies on the topic of annuities that have ultimately taken an opposite position to Wall Street's.

For instance, in 2006 and 2007 two professors from the Wharton Financial Institutions Center—David F. Babbel, professor of Insurance and Risk Management, the Wharton School of Business, and Craig B. Merrill, professor of Finance and Insurance, Brigham Young University—conducted a study that effectively countered many of the classic arguments against annuities. Actually, the study made a very good case in favor of them.

In this study, Babbel and Merrill first point out that there are "Five forces that are converging upon Americans in what some have called the Perfect Storm—others the Tsunami Wave—that is about to engulf us from all sides." The following numbered list is a paraphrase of the five forces they refer to:

1. *The decreasing levels and importance of Social Security:* The percentage of what we are projected to eventually receive in benefits, relative to what we contributed over the years, is staggeringly less than the benefits our parents received relative to their personal contribution.

2. *The demise of pensions and defined benefit plans:* According to their study, in 1983 there were 175,000 companies with pension plans; now there are fewer than 25,000 companies that still offer pensions. Making matters worse, the government's

Pension Benefit Guarantee Corporation (PBGC), the insurance company responsible for paying retiree pensions in the event of company failure, is reeling from all the corporate bankruptcies of recent years. Given the underfunded state of pension funds discussed in chapter 4, the prognosis for company pensions and the PBGC is worrisome.

3. *The aging of the baby boom generation:* Baby boomers, on average, have not saved enough for their own retirements and will be more dependent upon government programs such as Social Security, which will not be able to support them.

4. *The emergence of the post boomers:* The children of boomers (called "post boomers," "echo boomers," or "Generation Y") will not only be burdened by trying to save and provide for their own futures; this population will also have to support the Social Security and Medicare costs of the boomers. There just aren't enough of them.

5. *Increasing longevity of the American population:* Life expectancy has increased due to better health care, more preventive health measures, and less physically demanding work environments.

When these five forces are combined with lower interest rates from bonds and potentially lower returns from stocks, you have the makings of a retirement income disaster. Add that to what is called the biggest financial risk of the twenty-first century—living too long—and you find yourself smack dab in the middle of the proverbial $64-million question: How do you live your Preferred Lifestyle and not outlive your money?

Babbel and Merrill's advice to "begin by annuitizing enough of your assets so that you can provide for 100 percent of your minimum acceptable level of retirement income" supports our rationale for Lifestyle Driven Investing. Babbel and Merrill believe this is the most viable way to secure income for many retirees. For those who have amassed a sufficient level of wealth, it might be possible to invest strictly in U.S. government securities (i.e., Treasury Inflation Protected Securities), but it is highly unlikely that this strategy will work for many retirees when yields are low.

To determine how much to annuitize, Babbel and Merrill say to begin with your monthly income need and subtract Social Security, pension benefits, and any other retirement income you may receive. Sound familiar? This is very close to the calculation mentioned earlier in this book. They then suggest you annuitize a sufficient amount of your assets to provide the balance of the monthly income you will need.

The question you will need to ask yourself is: Do the advantages outweigh the restrictions? The following list paraphrases the two professors' excellent outline of the facts:

1. When you annuitize a policy and receive a payment, you are not taxed on 100 percent of the income you receive—only a part. You receive what is called the exclusion ratio, that is, a portion the IRS deems to be a return of your original investment. Thus, there is an excluded amount and a taxable amount in every payment that must be calculated and accounted for on your individual tax return.

2. While many forms of annuitizing do not allow for an increase in monthly income, some companies offer features

(or riders) that provide for an annual cost of living increase tied to the consumer price index, or CPI.

3. Your monthly income will likely be based on your age and sex using the insurance mortality tables. For older people, the income from an immediate annuity can sometimes be much higher than what they could find in the bond or fixed income markets. However, the downside is that their heirs might not receive the benefit of what could have been left over in another type of investment.

4. Since in many annuitization cases your heirs will not receive a death benefit, some people offset that by using a portion of the monthly income to purchase a life insurance policy to replace what the heirs would have lost.

5. The safety of an immediate or income annuity (the type we have discussed so far) is only as good as the claims-paying ability of the insurance company backing the obligation. That being said, insurance companies are required by law to set aside reserves, and insurance commissioners monitor these reserve requirements in every state in which the companies do business.

6. Once you have engaged in a contract and have begun taking income distributions there is generally no availability to receive lump sums in the case of an emergency. An annuity acts very much like a company pension plan, and many people realize they cannot go to the company and ask for an advance or a lump sum in lieu of payments.

This Wharton study describes only one type of annuity built around the decades-old structure of annuitization. While this may be the right solution for some people, there are other methods for receiving income from these products as well. My goal is to draw back the curtain on all the options so that you can decide for yourself. But before we get into the specifics of the various annuities that exist and their features and benefits, I want to take a minute to discuss *why* someone might want to pay extra for the guarantees offered by annuities. Why not just invest in stocks, bonds, mutual funds, or exchange-traded funds (ETFs) to provide for your retirement? Why pay extra for insurance? The reason seems obvious to me, yet I rarely hear it discussed.

WHY INSURE YOUR INVESTMENT PORTFOLIO?

In all areas of our life, insurance affords us the ability to transfer to someone else the risk of something bad occurring to us. We purchase homeowner's insurance to transfer the risk of rebuilding our home in the event it burns down. We buy car insurance to transfer the risk of accident and injury. The same goes for health insurance, life insurance, disability insurance, and long-term care insurance. That is the simple reason we buy insurance of any kind: to transfer the risk of a catastrophic loss from ourselves to someone else—in many cases, an insurance company.

Sometimes when I think about this and how conditioned we are to buying all types of insurance, I think about some of our wealthier clients and chuckle at the idea of them buying comprehensive automobile insurance. Many of our clients have the financial resources to purchase an entire car dealership, so they certainly would not miss a meal if their car were totaled. Yet they are financially savvy individuals and realize there is great leverage in paying a small amount of money in terms of monthly premiums rather than risk paying out a large amount to replace a car in the event of an accident.

Now let's transfer this concept to the idea of "insuring" our investment portfolios. In traditional terms, many of us plan to work thirty-five to forty years and save and accumulate funds that we hope will ultimately be sufficient to sustain our lifestyle until we die. Many of us do not count on inheritances or other financial windfalls. What we have when we retire is usually only what we have saved, and that is it.

Outside of entitlement programs like Social Security, or in rare cases a pension, that nest egg becomes the financial work-horse, the sole source of income that we depend on to provide for our needs for the rest of our lives. What I find fascinating is that more people do not think about insuring the workhorse. If the workhorse breaks a leg (i.e., the portfolio declines substantially in value), it could certainly have a direct and immediate impact on your ability to live your life and enjoy your lifestyle.

As I speak to financial advisors throughout the country, I remind them that in our profession we all advise our clients to buy and maintain many forms of insurance—homeowner's, automobile, long-term care, etc. That goes without saying. But I also point out that the odds are statistically low that a client's home will burn to the ground, and if it did, the capital outlay required to rebuild it would be finite.

By contrast, the odds are exceptionally high—as we have recently witnessed—that sometime during our clients' years of retirement, which can last forty years or more, their investment portfolios will take a massive hit in terms of the underlying value available to sustain their lifestyles. On a relative basis, the cost of replacing your home or your auto would be *substantially* less than rebuilding the size of an investment portfolio required to sustain your lifestyle. For some of you, it took forty years to accumulate your nest egg—and for some, about three weeks to lose half of it. Many of us know retirees who watched their investment portfolios burn to the ground during the 2008 financial crisis. Wouldn't it have been nice for them to have had some insurance on their investment portfolio? How do they replace what was lost in terms of the asset base to produce their income? The issue of insuring your investments is very important and something every person should seriously consider.

Many financial advisors believe the protection offered by annuities is unnecessary; they think they know how to time the markets. Unfortunately, although these advisors may be very bright, I believe they are simply playing an unwinnable game. More troubling is the idea that in a down market you could have an advisor who consistently "beats the market" yet you could still end up running out of money. The advisor, for example, could be downright proud of himself for being down *only* 30 percent when the market is down 45 percent. That would be the description of an advisor or manager who has essentially beaten the market. No matter how you spin it, the end result of trying to beat the market essentially does nothing to prepare for or preserve your Preferred Lifestyle.

Could the markets have three or four back-to-back years of being down? It has certainly happened before. My bottom line is that if it could happen again, I do not want to be at the wrong end of the bet!

The guarantees offered by annuities are a direct form of insurance. The insurance company is insuring your ability to maintain a predetermined stream of income for a set amount of time: in some cases, the rest of your life.

Of course, in all cases, this assumes that the insurance company with whom you do business remains solvent. The issue of solvency shouldn't keep you awake at night, however, because insurance companies are required to set aside reserves to meet their future payment requirements. Furthermore, insurance commissioners monitor those reserve requirements in all of the states where the insurance companies do business. In addition, many states guarantee annuities up to a certain level based on a formula developed within the office of the state insurance commissioner, which is supported annually by a portion of taxes or premiums related to the insurance companies doing business in that state. I have to admit, when I think about the current financial situation of the U.S. government and its *lack* of reserves, I see a strong argument for putting my money with an insurance company that is *required* to keep reserves.

With that in mind, let's take a look at the various annuities that exist in the marketplace today and how they can be used to insure at least a portion of your retirement income.

FIXED ANNUITIES

Fixed annuities provide the investor with a fixed rate of return over the holding period. The fixed rate of return is either paid out as income or reinvested to provide simple or compounded interest.

Though the tax and legal structures vary significantly, fixed annuities share some important characteristics with certificates of deposit (CDs). In fact, they can be viewed as competing products. The decision to choose one over the other will largely depend on the interest rates being offered and the safety of the underlying contract. Fees are not an issue since, in both cases, the interest rate received is net of fees, but other issues such as surrender charges or early withdrawal penalties should be considered.

Given the same rate of return, why might someone choose a fixed annuity over a CD? Confidence in the issuer might be a consideration. A second consideration might be the asset/creditor protection that certain states give to annuities. For instance, my state of Texas offers protection from creditors with respect to insurance contracts. A third consideration is the fact that an annuity contract offers tax deferral of earnings while many CDs and other financial instruments have taxes due as the interest is received or accrued.

As with every financial product, there are advantages and disadvantages to fixed annuities. Let's look at both lists for fixed annuities.

Advantages	Disadvantages
• Simple to understand and use	• Penalties for early withdrawals
• Income is guaranteed for life	• Income payments are taxed as ordinary income
• Death benefit is guaranteed	
• Annuities can be creditor protected*	• General asset of the insurance company
• Insurers are required to maintain reserves	• Insurers may "reinsure"**

* Annuities may be creditor protected, but that is based on your state's law. Review the laws in your state to determine whether annuities are a protected asset class.

** Insurers may reinsure their obligations with other insurance carriers. This can become problematic if your annuity purchase decision is based on the financial health of Insurer A and Insurer A sells your risk exposure to another carrier.

EQUITY-INDEXED ANNUITIES

Equity-indexed annuities (EIAs) are a form of fixed annuity. The biggest difference is that EIAs have a stock market component to them. As the name suggests, the stock market component is based on one or more indices, such as the S&P 500. The insurance company agrees to grow your investment either by a stated annual interest rate or by a percentage of the growth of the index chosen, whichever is greater. Before we go any further, let's define a few terms specific to equity-indexed annuities.

Participation rate: Since EIAs have a stock market component based on a market index, the participation rate defines how much gain in the index will be credited to the annuity. For example, if you have a participation rate of 80 percent and there is a 10 percent growth in the index, you would be credited with 8 percent, not the 10 percent growth.

Cap rate: Many EIAs limit the amount of growth you can have in your contract in a given year. This upper limit is referred to as a "cap." If in the example above you had a cap rate of 7 percent, your account would only be credited with 7 percent versus 8 percent gain. In a year when the index is negative, you would receive the annual interest rate stated in the policy, typically 0–3 percent.

The big selling point for equity-indexed annuities is that many of them guarantee at least your original principal, which can be very attractive, especially in this day and age. In addition, they promise to lock in your gains, whether that is the fixed interest rate or a higher participation rate based on stock market performance. One thing you need to consider with EIAs is surrender charges and surrender periods. A surrender charge is a charge that gets applied to withdrawals within a stated time period after making an investment. The industry had been criticized for having large surrender charges extending over a long period of time, which is one argument the opponents often cited. However, it should be noted that the insurance industry has made significant improvements in this area, and some companies now have much shorter surrender periods than we saw in contracts even ten years ago. I am heartened by this category of annuity because they seem to be making the greatest strides in features and benefits. As of this writing, EIAs tend to be more viable for the accumulation stage of life when someone is looking to let their money sit and grow for several years. I am hopeful the insurance industry will continue to improve upon equity indexed annuities in the days to come as they are a viable investment for someone to consider for a portion of their lifestyle money.

Here is a consolidated list of the primary advantages and disadvantages of equity-indexed annuities as I see them today:

Advantages	Disadvantages
• Provide some ability for stock market participation • Many offer guarantees of original principal • Creditor protection in some states • Good for accumulators who do not need income • Good for long-term investors who want principal guarantees	• Features and benefits can be confusing • Subject to the claims-paying ability of the insurance company; your money becomes a general asset of the insurance company, hence, company selection is crucial • Caps on market participation often limit your upside potential • Ability to receive income from these products varies widely by company • Sometimes long surrender periods and high surrender penalties for early withdrawal

VARIABLE ANNUITIES

Variable annuities are another way of securing a portion of your lifestyle income. I will start by saying if ever there was an investment vehicle that had been maligned by Wall Street, the prize would have to go to variable annuities. I will also admit that, prior to 1999, I agreed with most of the mainstream arguments against them. But in keeping with my position as a product agnostic, I kept my eyes open and discovered some great applications for these vehicles. My goal here is to explain them in as much detail as feasibly possible, give you the pros and cons, and discuss why they may or may not fit into your Lifestyle portfolio. Please keep in mind, variable annuities are very different from fixed annuities and should not be thought of as a competing product. If anything, variable annuities compete with mutual funds, and the costs of a variable annuity should be weighed against the value of any guarantees received from it.

Once again, let's start by defining a few terms that are particularly relevant to variable annuities.

Terminology Bank

Variable annuity: Just like the other annuities we have discussed, this is also a contract with an insurance company. The word "variable" describes how the funds (premium payments) are invested. Rather than having a fixed rate of return (fixed annuity) or being based on a broad index (equity-indexed annuity), a variable annuity allows you to invest in a wide variety of pooled investment accounts similar in many ways to mutual funds. These accounts, called "subaccounts" inside a variable annuity, range from highly aggressive to very conservative. A variable annuity gives you many more investment options than any other type of annuity.

Rider: This is a term used to describe an optional benefit or feature available with an annuity. Many variable annuities have a number of riders available, allowing you to customize your annuity to fit your specific needs. The cost of the annuity depends greatly on the number of riders you select.

Enhanced death benefit: This is an example of a rider that can be added to an annuity contract, and it provides a payout to the annuitant's beneficiaries after he or she dies. This rider functions much like life insurance would except that there is no underwriting required and the amount of death benefit is often linked in some way to the performance of the annuity value.

Living benefit: This is another rider that can be added to a variable annuity contract. Unlike the death benefit, the living benefit offers the annuitant benefits *during* his or her lifetime. It guarantees at least a minimum rate of growth during the accumulation phase and then guarantees a rate of income during the distribution phase. To fully understand this concept you need to think back to our discussion about annuitization. Remember, annuitization refers to regular payments for the duration of the annuitant's life. There are a couple of major differences between annuitization and a living benefit:

1. When you annuitize a sum of money, there is usually no death benefit. A living benefit allows a person to get income payments for life and potentially still leave a death benefit to his or her beneficiaries, assuming the subaccount value does not go to zero.

2. With annuitization, the income payments are generally fixed: there is typically no opportunity for them to go down or up (although, as stated before, there have been a few product designs that include a cost of living adjustment). A living benefit provides a way for you to get income without annuitization, which provides the opportunity for you to get an increase in income (or what I refer to as "getting a raise"). Remember, whether the income is from annuitization or a living benefit, it still depends on the claims-paying ability of the insurer.

Guaranteed income base: This very important term is used in conjunction with a living benefit. The guaranteed income base (GIB) is the value on which the income from the living benefit is based. The reason this is so important is because it is guaranteed. One reason some people don't like variable annuities is because of their variable nature; in other words, the value of the mutual funds you choose can go up or down in value. However, the GIB is guaranteed by the insurance company not to go down, although the performance of the underlying investments (the mutual fund subaccounts) can *increase* its value. This leads us to the next term we need to define.

Step-up: A step-up is a feature included in the living benefits of some variable annuities that provides for a potential increase in the value of the GIB. The guaranteed income base automatically grows by at least the minimum rate of growth stated in the living benefit but has the opportunity to "step-up" to a higher value if the underlying investments (subaccounts) outperform the minimum rate of growth. A huge factor that differentiates variable annuities from fixed annuities or equity-indexed annuities is that there is no cap on the growth of the GIB; there is literally unlimited upside potential. While certainly not indicative of future performance, I have personally seen variable annuity contracts with over 30 percent gains in the account value and GIB in only one year.

Lock-in: A lock-in refers to a point in time at which the insurance company guarantees that the GIB will not go any lower than its present value. This is very important because if you have a step-up in value, you want the insurance company to guarantee that new higher value for income purposes! The time frame for lock-ins can vary significantly from company to company. Some will lock-in your GIB values on an annual basis, some will lock-in quarterly, and some will even give you daily lock-ins.

To me, the step-up and the lock-in features are probably the most important benefits of a variable annuity, and what was missing in annuities created prior to 1999. Without these two features, I could understand why some advisors were reluctant to recommend this type of annuity to their clients versus a mutual fund or other type of investment. They have definitely been key enhancements to variable annuity products.

Let me point out one thing just to make sure we are all on the same page: the GIB should not be confused with the account value of the annuity. The account value is the total value of all the subaccounts you choose to invest in, and the subaccounts can go either up or down in value. In a variable annuity contract with a living benefit, the insurance company is not guaranteeing your account value; that will fluctuate with the market, based on your subaccount selections. It is guaranteeing the income base and the income payments calculated from the income base. If, for whatever reason, you decide to cash out your account, you will receive only the value of the underlying subaccounts, not the GIB value.

In a variable annuity contract, the insurance company is not guaranteeing your account value; that will fluctuate with the market, based on your subaccount selections. It is guaranteeing the income base and the income payments calculated from the income base.

A Real-life Story

The real test of any investment is how it performs when the rubber meets the road. Now that you have a basic understanding of the mechanics and terminology surrounding variable annuities, I want to tell you a real-life story about how a variable annuity with a guaranteed income benefit worked out for one of our clients. I will refer to her as "Janey Black."

Janey and her husband, Tony, first came to our firm in the early '90s. Janey was an accomplished CPA and Tony had retired several years earlier from a pharmaceutical company. Because I rarely recommended variable annuities before 1999, the Blacks' portfolio did not include any. But, as I've mentioned a time or two before, I try to be as objective as possible and change my opinions as the facts change.

The first living benefit riders came to the market sometime in 1999 (or at least that's when I became aware of them). After a thorough study of a specific product, I recommended during one of our meetings in early 2000 that Janey and Tony take a portion of their investment portfolio and invest it in this specific variable annuity with a living benefit. The living benefit from that company guaranteed them a minimum 5 percent annual growth of the GIB or the market value, whichever was higher, during the accumulation phase, and a 5 percent income stream from the GIB during the distribution phase. They were a little taken aback that my stance had changed so dramatically, but when I gave them my rationale and the evidence, they agreed that the new information warranted a new look and consideration. They liked what they saw, and ended up investing $1 million in this product.

During the years of the tech wreck, the Blacks only benefited from the 5 percent growth of the GIB. They were very happy about that, though, because the balance of their portfolio that had not been invested in variable annuities had gone down relative to the rest of the markets.

In the early 2000s, Tony lost a long battle with cancer and

passed away. Fortunately, Janey was able to live on his pension benefits and didn't have to touch her variable annuity.

As we can all attest, the markets in the decade of the 2000s went down, then up, and then down again, with the Dow Jones Industrial Average peaking somewhere around 14,000 in November 2007. The living benefit on Janey's variable annuity guaranteed her a 5 percent annual growth of the GIB or the value of her subaccounts, whichever was higher. Additionally, it locked in the higher of the two values on an annual basis. Sometime in the year 2007, when the stock market was high, Janey's subaccounts grew to a value higher than her original GIB, so her GIB stepped-up to that level and locked in there.

Sometime in November 2008, shortly after the infamous market collapse, Janey called my office and requested a meeting. She had an adult son with a debilitating illness who was going to have to quit work despite having four children and a wife to support. Janey wanted to see how she could help him financially. On the phone, Janey made the comment, "I know this is a horrible time in the market to have this discussion." And it was—the market had completely collapsed two months prior. But when she made that comment, I realized that Janey had absolutely no idea what she really owned in terms of the variable annuity.

Janey came in and we chatted about her family, particularly the medical issue with her son. It was clear he needed to quit work, and she wanted to help as much as she could. "How much do you want to be able to give him?" I asked.

She answered, "I'd like to be able to give him $1,000 a month."

In surprise, I repeated it back to her. "A thousand dollars a month? So you are talking about $12,000 a year?" I couldn't imagine how that little amount of money could help a family of six.

Janey looked crestfallen. "Do you think that is too much?"

"Janey," I said, "your guaranteed income base locked in last year at $2.2 million. By contract, you are able to take out 5 percent of that minimum income base annually for the rest of your life. That is $110,000 a year."

Janey started to cry. "I had no idea," she said, absolutely stunned. "I had no idea."

Now, keep in mind that had she come in and requested that we just cash out her remaining value in these annuity contracts, I would not have been able to deliver such good news. Remember, the insurance company guarantees the GIB, not your account value. Thus, the cash-out value is always the market value, which in Janey's case had declined along with the rest of the stock market and was much less than $2.2 million. Needless to say, she started taking the income and did *not* cash out. The point is the periodic lock-ins of the GIB gave this woman the chance to help her son, at least for the rest of her natural life. And based on the contract she had purchased, there was also a chance some kind of death benefit would be available when she passed away.

Of course, all of this is based on the claims-paying ability of the underlying insurance company, which is obviously a very important consideration. That said, had Janey kept that $1 million invested outside of a variable annuity for all of those years, she certainly wouldn't have had the ability to help her son nearly as much as she has been able to since having that conversation.

As this story illustrates, a variable annuity can provide an investor with a way to insure an income stream for the rest of the investor's life without capping upside potential.

Another True Story

Let me tell you one more story, this time of a couple who decided *not* to insure a portion of their retirement income. Our clients, who I'll refer to as "Larry and Jan Smith," were getting ready to retire at the age of sixty-two. They had accumulated a portfolio of around $2 million and their basic lifestyle called for about $100,000 in income (5 percent of their portfolio). When they met with us, we discussed using living benefits within variable annuities to transfer the risk of running out of money before running out of time. Because of the fees and a few other issues, Larry and Jan decided to stay with their mutual fund portfolio, which they held at a large brokerage house, and just take out systematic withdrawals of $100,000 per year. They decided to contract with us to help them with their estate planning and overall retirement modeling but not to manage their investment portfolio. The date of our initial meeting was in early 2000.

Can you guess what happened? After just twelve months in retirement, their $2,000,000 portfolio was down to $1,300,000 (the market had taken away $600,000, or 30 percent, and they had taken out $100,000 to live on). At their request, we sat down with them the next year and recommended that if they still intended to maintain their mutual fund portfolio, they needed to reduce their withdrawal amount to 5 percent of the lower market value of $1,300,000 (which would mean living on $65,000). Larry and Jan's response was, "Thank you for the advice, but we can't afford to take a 35 percent pay cut." Unfortunately, the next year (on the second anniversary of their retirement), their nest egg was worth less than half of the original balance. It didn't take a rocket scientist to figure out they were clearly at risk of running out of money at some point in the future.

Instead of reducing their lifestyle, however, Larry went back to work (literally as a greeter at Walmart) and the Smiths' dream retirement of travel and golf was gone, probably forever. In hindsight, the fees and expenses internal to the variable annuities we had recommended would have been insignificant relative to the guaranteed lifestyle the various annuities would have provided. The lesson to be learned: be careful not to be penny-wise and pound-foolish. It's a nasty world out there.

Advantages and Disadvantages of Variable Annuities

Like any financial instrument, variable annuities have their advantages and disadvantages. Clearly the biggest advantage investors cite is that variable annuities give them the chance to have the best of both worlds—exposure to the upside potential of the stock market, bond market, or international markets for future income purposes and assurance they will have an income stream, based on the GIB, for the rest of their lives.

Before we conclude this section, I want to compare and contrast variable annuities with the other types of annuities and give you a side-by-side comparison of the pros and cons.

Insurance Company Liability

A big difference between a variable annuity and a fixed or equity-indexed annuity is that a variable annuity does not commingle the investor's account with the general assets of the insurance company. This means that the investor retains ownership of the underlying values in the subaccounts at all times. This would be important if the insurance company ever filed for bankruptcy or went out of business. In a variable annuity, you could lose the

GIB the insurance company was insuring, but you would still own the subaccounts and could get that money back. Fixed or equity-indexed annuities, on the other hand, pool your money with that of other investors in the general accounts of the insurance company, which subjects them to the insurance company's creditors. If the insurance company were to go bankrupt or out of business, you would be considered a creditor of the insurance company. That being said, each state in which an insurance company does business has a fund set up to re-insure, up to a certain amount, your investment. You would need to check with your state insurance commissioner to determine the amount your state would guarantee.

Participation Rates and Caps

I already mentioned this briefly but wanted to point it out again since it is such a significant difference. A fixed annuity promises you a fixed rate of return so you know exactly what you are going to get, and it does not change. An equity-indexed annuity (EIA) offers a minimum rate of return or the growth of a market index, whichever is higher. However, you are only allowed to participate with the growth of the index at a certain participation rate, and your growth is capped at an annual maximum. Additionally, it needs to be pointed out that some of these contracts allow the company to change the participation and/or cap rates in the *middle* of your term. In a variable annuity you get to participate 100 percent in the growth of the subaccounts you select, and there is no limit to your growth.

Outside the insurance industry, we have not found any vehicle where the value of your portfolio would be "locked in" on an annual, quarterly, or daily basis for income or any other purpose. Variable annuities give you an income base, which is based on a minimum guaranteed rate of return or the stock market value—whichever is higher. That higher value is then locked in on a regular basis for future income purposes.

Fees

Fixed and equity-indexed annuities generally include a few "baked in" expenses. The expenses are factored into your return rate and the caps on your growth. This can be both good and bad. It is nice in the sense that you do not have to pay any out-of-pocket fees, but your opportunity cost could end up being higher. For example, if the index you were invested in grew by 20 percent one year and you were capped at 7 percent, your fee, the opportunity cost, would be essentially 13 percent that year. Of course, the positive is that you still get a minimum rate of return if the market is down. With a variable annuity there are annual fees that get paid out of your account value, and the fees vary depending on the number of features and riders you select. The fees do not affect your GIB, however, nor do they reduce the amount of your income payments.

In terms of regulatory oversight, variable annuities are classified as a "security"; therefore, any advisor selling them is required to have both an insurance license and a securities license, which means those who recommend VAs fall under the supervision of the Department of Insurance and the Financial Industry National Regulatory Authority (FINRA). This is in contrast with those who sell only fixed annuities and/or equity-indexed annuities because, as of the writing of this book, EIAs are not considered a "security," which means neither the Securities and Exchange Commission nor FINRA regulate them. They are regulated only by the Department of Insurance. For this reason, there is more regulation for those selling variable annuities than for those who sell only fixed or equity-indexed annuities.

Remember that variable annuities should be viewed as competing products with mutual funds. If your money is in mutual funds, you enjoy none of the above guarantees. Not only is your income not guaranteed but, if the markets plummet, you could lose principal as well. And if the value of your mutual funds goes to zero, you will have nothing to generate income with and nothing to leave your children.

Taxes

There are pros and cons in terms of tax consequences for variable annuities. In terms of comparing them to traditional mutual funds, managed accounts, or ETFs, one tax benefit is that they enjoy tax deferral of earnings during the accumulation phase. This can be especially valuable to someone who has a large portion of money currently in taxable investment accounts. However, one of the negatives often pointed out is that income distributed from annuities is taxed at ordinary income rates as opposed to capital gains tax treatment that could be available on mutual funds, ETFs, or stock portfolios. For those in higher income tax brackets, this could be a stumbling block, but many people mentally view this portion of their investment portfolio as similar to setting up their own pension. Income from a company pension would be taxed at ordinary income rates, so this is rarely an issue. What they do not find justifiable is significantly reducing their lifestyle due to a significant or sustained market correction. In their minds, losing their ability to sustain their lifestyle in terms of predictable income would be far more damaging to their psyche than paying ordinary income taxes, something they can easily factor into their plan.

I have noticed that my clients who are interested in variable annuities are happy to trade off potentially reduced tax benefits for the guarantee of their Preferred Lifestyle. If you are like many of my clients you might say something like, "I want my life-style guaranteed; my kids can worry about the taxes when I die." Because of the potential for a death benefit, which again is based on the claims-paying ability of the insurance company, your kids may at least get something to argue about.

Surrender Penalties

Surrender penalties are a reality of many insurance vehicles and depend on the insurer and the specific type of annuity. It is not unusual to have to leave your initial investment with the insurer from one to seven years or more before they completely waive penalties for cashing out your original principal. However, keep in mind that the insurance company does not charge a penalty for turning on the income. Surrender penalties are generally not a concern for our clients who choose to invest in variable annuities since they are generally a part of a longer-term income plan.

Asset Protection

Some states, such as my state of Texas, extend asset protection to annuity contracts, which means they are protected from creditors and bankruptcies. If you reside in a state with similar provisions, there is a chance that your assets would be protected from the claims of creditors or from claims resulting from a legal judgment against you. Of course, you should consult with appropriate advisors before drawing any conclusions about your state of residence. While you might not want to invest in these products solely for the purpose of asset protection, it may be a valuable by-product.

Probate

Annuities are not subject to probate. The probate process can be avoided through simple techniques on certain types of accounts, including the designation of a beneficiary. Annuities provide for just such an election, which if properly used will avoid probate at the death of the owner. That being said, any death benefit is included in the value of an estate for estate tax calculation purposes.

To conclude our discussion of variable annuities, here is a side-by-side comparison of the pros and cons as I see them today.

Pros	Cons
• Provide the ability to participate in the gains of the stock and bond markets	• Features and benefits can often be confusing
• A guaranteed GIB that can be stepped-up and locked-in	• The income guarantee is subject to the claims-paying ability of the insurance company
• No cap on upside potential	• Only your GIB is guaranteed, not your original principal
• Tax deferral of gains	
• Guarantees a lifetime worth of income without having to use annuitization	• Income is taxed at ordinary income rates
• Your money is not a "general asset" of the insurance company	• Fees can be higher than some other investment products, depending on the benefits selected
• The ability to elect a death benefit, regardless of insurability	

I believe that annuities with living income benefits can be appropriate and well suited for a portion of a retiree's Lifestyle portfolio. It is a shame that more advisors don't view these from their clients' point of view, but instead make every conceivable argument against this investment. All of the arguments they make are viable—tax treatment, cost, etc.—but if they really tried to get into the mind-set of the retiree, I think they would realize their clients just want to retire, spend time doing what they want to do, and create a sustainable lifestyle that is not going to be subject to the whims of the markets. And yes, many retirees are actually willing to pay a little more to get that.

At the end of the day, I want people to think for themselves and make decisions that support their financial needs, not to be swayed one way or another by an advisor with her own agenda. There have been times when a client has told me he ran the idea of buying an annuity past his stockbroker and the broker came up with all kinds of arguments, using every arrow she had in her objections quiver. Whenever I hear this, I lightheartedly tell the client to go back to the broker and see if she is okay with the client moving in with her if or when the client runs out of money. That usually changes the conversation!

A FINAL WORD ON ANNUITIES

While great annuity products have been created since 1999, I have no idea what type of products will exist at the time you are reading this book. As stated several times in this discussion, the underlying guarantees are only as good as the financial stability of the insurance company, so I would like to give you a resource you can use. One rating service I have used in the past can be found at www.ambest.com. This group tracks the underlying health of insurance companies, which is an important factor to consider.

It is worth noting variable annuity products tend to open up to the public and then close to new investors after a period of time. Normally, even after the product is closed to new investors, existing contract holders can add additional sums (sometimes up to $1 million per contract) and retain the terms of the original offering. When I find an offering that looks attractive, what I usually do is encourage my clients to open up a "place holder" with the minimum amount required to open a contract. Often this is $10,000. This locks in the terms of that offering for the investor, buying them time to identify additional funds they might want to invest and removing the risk of a product closing before their larger funds became available. If your intent is to add future 401(k) or other "qualified" dollars, you need to be sure you open the original contract with "qualified" dollars, which is usually IRA dollars from a previous rollover. There are tax implications to mixing some types of IRA dollars with 401(k) dollars, so be sure to check with your CPA so you are not commingling the wrong types of accounts. If you are working with non-IRA and/or non-401(k) dollars, you can open the place holders with money from your checking, savings, or brokerage accounts and add from those sources in the future.

THE BOTTOM LINE

The bottom line in determining whether any kind of annuity might be appropriate for you greatly depends on your desire to have some part of your retirement guaranteed. If you are looking for a guaranteed income stream, with potential for upside based on market participation, you might choose a variable annuity.* If you are looking to have your original principal guaranteed and have some, but not all, participation in the financial markets, an equity-indexed annuity might make sense.* If you want the greatest amount of income for the dollars invested, you might look into the classic life annuity option, which is similar to creating a personal pension.* (Keep in mind, with this last option, there may not be a death benefit available to your heirs. This may or may not be important to you.) In making these decisions, you should not ignore the trifecta of risks that exist in our world: longevity risk, inflation risk, and, as always, market risk. All of these risks are exacerbated for retirees who have a set amount of money to invest and live on for the rest of their lives.

Regardless of when you are reading this book, it is clear Congress and the marketplace in general are looking for ways to alleviate some of the risk of retirees running out of money before they run out of time. I am confident the demand for these types of products will not go away, and I am equally confident the marketplace will continue to fill the need!

*In all cases, the guarantees of any annuity are subject to the claims-paying ability of the underlying insurer.

ERIN'S ESSENTIALS

- Annuities, along with U.S. government securities, are the only investments that can legally be said to be "guaranteed." (Guarantees are based on the claims-paying ability of the underlying insurance company.)
- There are many types of annuities; it is important to evaluate an individual annuity by itself and to decide based on its own merits. Even within a specific insurance company, there may be one that fits and one that doesn't fit your needs.
- Annuities do not always have to be "annuitized" in order to secure an income stream.
- With the decrease in employee pensions, fixed, variable, and equity-indexed annuities have become popular income vehicles since the early 2000s.
- Buying an annuity is sometimes thought of as similar to creating a self-funded pension plan.
- **Ask yourself:**
  - Have I considered any type of annuity to help fund my retirement?
  - Have I done adequate research on the various types of annuities to rule them in or out of my portfolio?
  - Absent an annuity, is there any other way I can get guaranteed income?
  - Would my confidence about the future change if I knew I could have a certain amount of income that was certain to come in each and every month?

- Which insurance company would I trust to keep that promise?

For more information and complimentary reports, go to
www.thebigretirementrisk.com.

CHAPTER 10

HYBRID AND NON-LIFESTYLE INVESTMENTS

Now that we have talked in depth about a couple of potential Lifestyle investments, I want to introduce you to some financial products I currently have separated into the other two categories, Hybrid and Non-Lifestyle. While these products do not meet the criteria of Lifestyle investments, they may still merit a look when you are contemplating how best to invest the rest of your money.

HYBRID INVESTMENTS THAT PROVIDE CURRENT INCOME

Remember, a Hybrid investment may produce an income, but you could not claim that that income was safe or predictable or guaranteed. Other Hybrid products may have some form of guarantee, but they do not produce any income. Again, there is nothing inherently wrong with using a Hybrid investment to produce some of the cash flow for your basic Needs and Wants, but you must understand and accept that there is innately more risk involved. Your job is to identify the risks and decide what level of risk you are willing to accept.

A Hybrid investment may produce an income, but you could not claim that the income was safe or predictable or guaranteed.

Now that we've established our ground rules, let's take a look at the different kinds of Hybrid products available.

Managed Bond Portfolios

There are a couple of ways to buy bonds without buying the individual bonds themselves. The first is to invest in some form of managed bond portfolio. This could be a mutual fund or an exchange-traded fund (ETF).

Depending on how much you have to invest, you may not be able to get the appropriate or desired amount of diversification by purchasing individual bonds. The immediate diversification benefit of holding a managed portfolio of bonds provides some level of safety against the credit risk of an individual company defaulting on their bonds. In this case, you would own a fractional share of all the bonds held in the fund. It is conceivable that the default of one bond or a very small percentage of the bond portfolio might not have a devastating impact on the overall performance of the fund.

What you give up by investing in a bond fund is control over the selection of the bonds and any decisions about the rate, durations, and/or holding periods of the bonds. Since you do not control when bonds are bought or sold, a manager could sell them at a loss for a number of reasons. If there is a "run on the bank" and a number of investors want to cash out of the fund, the manager would be forced to sell enough bonds to provide for the liquidity need, regardless of whether or not the manager believes it is a good time to sell. The manager may also have to sell bonds at a loss in order to maintain a certain yield in comparison to the market. Whatever the cause, you could inadvertently be locking in losses.

While owning corporate and municipal bonds in a managed portfolio makes sense for some people, U.S. government securities are a different story. In this case, there is no diversification benefit because the bonds are all issued by the same entity, the U.S. government, and are considered credit-risk-free. In my opinion, the only reason anyone would buy a U.S. government security is for the guarantee that all interest and principal will be repaid; if you hold the bond to maturity, it gives you the highest degree of safety. If, however, you buy a mutual fund or managed portfolio of U.S. government securities, you virtually take away the guarantee of getting your entire principal back since the manager could sell bonds prior to maturity at a loss. Instead of owning one bond with one interest rate and maturity date, you would own a fractional interest in a large portfolio of bonds.

It is very difficult for a manager to protect the underlying principal value of a bond portfolio in a rising interest-rate environment. While the manager may be able to give you some increase in income in the portfolio by replacing lower-yielding bonds with higher-yielding bonds, the trade-off will be risk to the underlying principal value of the portfolio. Hence, I rarely recommend anyone buy a government bond mutual fund or managed portfolio. If you want safety, my recommendation is to buy the individual issue and plan to hold it to maturity.

Preferred Stock

Preferred stock is a very interesting investment with its own set of advantages and disadvantages. It is essentially a stock and bond mix. Preferred stock is like common stock in that it can receive dividends from the company, may participate in some upside if the company does well, and is lower in the capital structure than bonds—meaning preferred shareholders would receive money after the bondholders have been paid in the event the company goes bankrupt. However, preferred stock is also like a bond in that it is higher in the capital structure than common stock, meaning preferred stockholders receive their dividends before common stockholders. Also like a bond, the price of preferred shares is more influenced by changes in interest rates than by the performance of the underlying company.

The key here is that preferred stock provides a dividend stream that is fairly consistent. Unlike a bond, preferred stock generally has no maturity so the owner can hold it indefinitely, which is good if the company is strong and the dividend rate is high. This is bad if interest rates are low and are expected to increase because preferred stock is much more sensitive to changes in interest rates than are bonds.

Preferred stock also does not typically have voting power like common shareholders. This is usually irrelevant, as many investors do not vote in person or via proxy due to the relatively small impact their voting has on elections and their lack of knowledge regarding the candidates for election.

Lastly, preferred stock can have what is known as a cumulative feature. This means that any reduction or elimination of dividends to preferred shareholders must be completely paid up before the company can begin making any dividend payments to common stockholders. For example, if you purchased one share of preferred stock for $100, with a stated dividend rate of 6 percent, that share should generate $6 per year in dividends paid to you. But if the company were to hit hard times and could not pay the dividend at all for two years, you would receive no dividend—hence the lack of a safe, predictable, or guaranteed income stream. If, after two years, the company were able to start paying a dividend again, they would have to pay you the dividends you should have received on your cumulative preferred stock during those two years ($12) as well as the current year's dividend ($6) before beginning to pay dividends to the common shareholders.

Preferred stock, as you can see, is an interesting investment that can have many uses. It can provide an income stream in the form of dividends, but the dividend can be suspended at the discretion of the company. There are additional risks associated with preferred stock, most importantly, interest-rate risk. As rates increase, the preferred stock value will tend to decrease.

Preferred stock can be purchased outright or through mutual funds and ETFs for diversification. While it certainly has its advantages, preferred stock is not an asset class we use or recommend very often; there are too many variables even for a Hybrid.

> While it certainly has its advantages,
> preferred stock is not an asset class
> we use or recommend very often;
> there are too many variables
> even for a Hybrid.

Publicly Traded REITs

We discussed Non-Listed/Non-Traded Real Estate Investment Trusts (REITs) in detail in chapter 8. Publicly Traded REITs, on the other hand, generally do not fit our Lifestyle category because of the risks associated with this type of investment. Due to the fact that many Publicly Traded REITs do produce income in the form of a dividend, they may be categorized as a Hybrid investment, but you must be aware that the underlying value of the stock can fluctuate drastically.

Publicly Traded REITs generally provide above-market income potential, allow for liquidity (they are easily traded on the open market), and have price appreciation potential. These REITs can be traded like any stock or ETF through a broker, either online or through their branch.

The main issue I see with Publicly Traded REITs is that the market price of the security fluctuates based on the whims and emotions of investors and the stock market as a whole. For this reason, the value of a Publicly Traded REIT often does not coincide with the true value of the underlying assets. My position on Publicly Traded REITs is if you are able to find a REIT manager with a significant management track record of stable and/or rising dividend income, and you are absolutely certain you will not be swayed by day-to-day market price fluctuations, then you might consider a Publicly Traded REIT as a viable Hybrid investment. If, however, you are going to be unduly nervous if the share value of the REIT declines significantly then I would remove it from your consideration as a viable Hybrid investment choice.

Covered Calls

If you have never heard of a covered call, you are not alone. Covered calls are really an investment technique that can be used to generate income from a stock position. If you have a large concentration of a single publicly traded stock, you might consider a covered call investment strategy to produce income from that existing stock position. This income can be used to subsidize the cash flow coming from other sources, such as a pension, Social Security, and income from your Lifestyle investments.

A common situation where a covered call strategy makes sense is when a person soon to be a retiree has a high concentration in a single publicly traded stock. After he sells off a sufficient number of shares to reposition into Lifestyle investments, there may be additional shares available, which we often call "legacy" stock. The client has no reason to sell, nor intention of selling, the remaining shares because his lifestyle income has already been satisfied. In some cases, he will agree to enter into a covered call program using his legacy stock to generate additional income for nonessential uses. A risk that is ever present in a covered call writing program is the risk of having your stock sold (or called away) if you are not paying attention. This can be devastating from a tax perspective if the legacy stock was comprised of very low basis shares.

Because the complexity of this strategy is beyond the scope of this book, I will not discuss it in any detail here. Suffice it to say, selling covered calls can be a viable strategy for either creating income or increasing the amount of income produced by a large stock position. Like other strategies, it has its pros and cons and should be entered into only after careful consideration of the risks that could be involved.

Master Limited Partnerships

Like covered calls, master limited partnerships (MLPs) are also not very well known, though this is beginning to change. MLPs are essentially limited partnerships that invest in a variety of energy-related opportunities. They combine the tax benefits of a limited partnership with the liquidity of publicly traded securities.

To qualify for MLP status, the partnership must generate at least 90 percent of its income from what the Internal Revenue Service deems "qualifying" sources. These include all manner of activities related to the production, processing, and transportation of oil, natural gas, and coal. Some real estate enterprises may also qualify as MLPs.

Because of such stringent requirements, the vast majority of MLPs are pipeline businesses, which earn relatively stable incomes from the transport of oil, gasoline, or natural gas. Like REITs, MLPs pay out most of their excess cash flow to unit holders each quarter. Most pride themselves on their ever-increasing dividend yield, which can be attractive to retirees. For reasons that exceed the scope of this book, however, MLPs are usually not attractive for IRAs/tax-deferred dollars.

A big benefit of MLPs is the cash flow. In practice, MLPs pay their investors through quarterly required distributions (QRDs), the amount of which is stated in the contract between the limited partners (the investors) and the general partner (the managers). These dividends often exceed other forms of traditional income, and failure to pay the QRD may constitute an event of default. In addition, the dividends from MLPs often receive special tax treatment. A portion of the dividend is generally treated as a return of capital, which means you will not owe income tax on the entire dividend. For example, let's assume you purchase an MLP unit for $100 that pays a 10 percent dividend and 90 percent of the dividend is treated as a return of capital. In this case, you would receive $10 from the MLP as a dividend but only pay tax on $1 since the other $9 would be treated as a return of your capital.

Other advantages of MLPs include a historically lower correlation to the stock and bond markets. Because of their unique infrastructure, MLPs even have a low correlation to the price of the actual commodities that travel through their pipelines. More and more mutual funds and ETFs are beginning to invest in MLPs, and they could provide a viable income solution, especially in a low-interest-rate environment.

High-Dividend-Paying Stocks

No stock market investment can ever truly be considered a Lifestyle investment because the income—if it pays income—cannot credibly be said to be safe, predictable, or guaranteed. Dividends are often the first thing to get cut when a company falls on hard times. Banks have traditionally paid high dividends; however, during the 2008 crisis, the value of some banks fell to zero and the dividends paid by the sector as a whole were cut substantially.

That said, some sectors are safer and more predictable than others. Utilities, for example, tend to pay very consistent dividends. It is also rare for a utility to go bankrupt, though it certainly can happen. Many companies in other sectors have long traditions of paying and raising their dividends every year. In fact, there are several new indices (e.g., the Dividend Achievers Index and the Dividend Aristocrats Index) that include only companies that have raised their dividends for many consecutive years.

If you do not need income at the time, dividends can also be reinvested in new shares of stock, which can compound the growth of your investment nest egg. When you are ready to begin receiving the income, you simply "turn off" the reinvestment and take the dividends as cash.

For investors who want income with the possibility of capital gains, a diversified portfolio of stocks with growing dividends can be a substantial piece of your portfolio—assuming you have already met your Needs with Lifestyle investments, of course.

Other Income-Producing Hybrid Investments

We are constantly on the lookout for interesting income investment opportunities that would fit into our definition of "Hybrid." Some examples of these might be investments in private debt offerings, mezzanine debt structures, equipment leasing, investments in self-storage units, and other offerings one would generally not find in the large brokerage houses. Why? Because the offerer may only be looking to raise a relatively small amount of capital ($25 to $50 million), which would not lend itself to the large firms who have to satisfy the appetites of thousands of brokers and clients. That being said, it is in these smaller offerings we have found many hybrid opportunities and upon which we spend a large amount of time and due diligence. It must also be noted these offerings have their own set of risk parameters which must be weighed and considered; these are definitely not "risk free" investments.

HYBRID INVESTMENTS THAT DO NOT PROVIDE CURRENT INCOME

Over the years, we have found other types of investments that do not offer any type of income, but they do offer some sort of principal guarantee, which is obviously only as good as the underlying guarantor. For the purposes of this book, I will not go into these types of investments, but they do exist and we have used them in specific instances. Suffice it to say the financial markets and offerings are ever changing—Wall Street is beginning to get the idea investors want more certainty in their lives, so we are slowly seeing product manufacturers come to the marketplace with either income guarantees or principal guarantees. However, you will rarely see both.

NON-LIFESTYLE INVESTMENTS

Non-Lifestyle investments include *everything* not discussed in the Lifestyle and Hybrid sections. This is an important category because anything you have left over after providing for your lifestyle could be invested in more growth-oriented investments based on your risk tolerance.

As is probably clear by now, I am an advocate of beginning with Lifestyle investing and building a foundation of income designed so that you will not run out of income before you run out of time. Once this foundation is in place and you want to add a little risk but are still looking for income-producing investments, I suggest adding Hybrid investments to your portfolio. Once your lifestyle is taken care of, you can focus on investing for growth, creating your legacy, and perhaps a more comfortable lifestyle.

The investment options available in the Non-Lifestyle category are almost infinite. These would include investments such as individual stocks, stock mutual funds, separately managed accounts, ETFs, international stocks and funds, commodities, oil and gas, gold coins or bullion, and many others. Many of these investments provide potential for longer-term growth and capital appreciation; they just need to be thought of in a different light and have a much longer time horizon.

Non-Lifestyle investments are a very important part of an overall investment portfolio, but since there have been so many books written on these traditional forms of growth investing, I will not take the time to elaborate on them in this book. The main thing I want to emphasize is that Non-Lifestyle investments should be kept in their proper perspective and, for retirees, used only once you have locked down your essential lifestyle income.

You should now have a good idea of what we look for in terms of characteristics to identify financial instruments to consider for your Lifestyle, Hybrid, and Non-Lifestyle investments. While this is certainly not an exhaustive list, hopefully it has given you a better understanding of the purpose of each category and will help you assess the suitability and viability of the investments available to you at the time you read this. As you begin your journey of product selection, it is important that you are able to clearly identify the behavioral characteristics of whatever instrument you are considering. I want you to be able to look at every investment going forward and put it into one of the three categories: Lifestyle, Hybrid, or Non-Lifestyle. I also want you to have realistic expectations on how that investment will behave in various market circumstances so you are not surprised. More than anything else, I want you to be relatively certain, once your portfolio has been established, you will not run out of money before you run out of time!

Now let's look at a few of the risks that can ruin your day and how you can work to avoid them.

ERIN'S ESSENTIALS

- The world of Hybrid and Non-Lifestyle investments is nearly limitless.
- Many hybrid investments produce higher levels of current income than do bonds or other traditional investments.
- Most traditional investments held by investors today would likely fall into the Hybrid and Non-Lifestyle categories; either they don't produce an income or the income would likely not be considered safe or predictable or guaranteed.
- What is most important about any of the categories is to understand what to expect from that investment and what *not* to expect. For instance, if you invest in a traditional Non-Lifestyle investment, don't expect to get a secured income for life. Conversely, if you invest in a Lifestyle investment, don't expect to necessarily double or triple your money in a short amount of time.
- Each investment class has a role to play in your portfolio; some provide current lifestyle income; others can provide opportunities for significant growth.
- When retiring, don't put the cart before the horse; secure your income first, then focus on capital appreciation opportunities in the marketplace.
- **Ask yourself:**
  - What Hybrid and Non-Lifestyle investments do I currently own?
  - Are my returns high enough for the amount of risk I am taking in these areas?

- Am I wrongly assuming I can get secured income for life through some combination of the traditional investments I own (such as mutual funds, ETFs, or individual stocks)?

For more information and complimentary reports, go to **www.thebigretirementrisk.com**.

CHAPTER 11

OTHER RISKS THAT CAN RUIN YOUR DAY

Most people think financial planning starts and stops with investment planning. It should not. In fact, in my practice, investment planning and the selection of appropriate products occurs as a third or fourth step. In my opinion, everyone needs to go through some kind of risk assessment and risk management process, usually on a recurring basis.

Why do I put risk management in front of all other planning issues? Because life has a tricky little way of throwing barbs at us when we least expect them. Risks come in many forms, from financial and business risks to legal risk and moral obligations, such as needing to support a family member. What I have found is that if you start with identifying common risks that can occur, you can alleviate a lot of pain and aggravation if and when something actually does happen. By addressing the possibility of a risk, you can find potential solutions in a calm and rational manner. Trying to accomplish this after an event has occurred is nearly impossible; the damage has already been done.

For instance, if you are diagnosed with an illness it becomes almost impossible to buy long-term care or life insurance. What if one of your children is in a car accident, driving a vehicle in your name and covered by your automobile insurance? If someone is injured or dies as a result of the accident, the paper trail of ownership can lead the plaintiff's legal counsel back to you. Once the accident has occurred, it could be virtually impossible to extricate yourself from legal liability. Any attempt to protect yourself by moving your assets would likely be considered a fraudulent transfer and would be futile in virtually any court system.

In this chapter, we will look at the most common risks you may encounter. You may be familiar with some of these risks; others may surprise you. My goal is for you to be fully prepared for as many risks as possible so as to limit the number of surprises.

RISK MANAGEMENT 101

Despite the plethora of risks that are simply a part of daily life, there is much you can do in advance to plan for unforeseen events. The problem is many people never do the appropriate type of risk management planning. Why? They simply don't want to deal with it. In their mind, it's negative, and there is almost a phobia about creating what might become a self-fulfilling prophecy.

Identifying and managing risk issues are not skills taught in the major wealth management firms. For their own risk management reasons, they don't want to go on record with observations about risk management issues that would make them legally responsible for providing adequate recommendations to mitigate those risks. For this reason, I rarely see the type of risk management issues addressed that I believe are important.

From my criticism above, you might guess that risk management is an area about which I am rather passionate. You would be correct. Since I have had many personal experiences that could be described as "train wrecks," I have a natural propensity to look for the other shoe to drop when it comes to my clients' situations. While it may sound pessimistic, I see this as the most important step in our process. Even if you hired a talented money manager who doubled your money in a short period of time, it wouldn't make any difference if an event were to happen that took it all away. Without proper risk management, successful investments only give you more to lose.

Because of how much I focus on the area of risk management, I have received my highest compliments and thanks from clients who have benefited from my being proactive in their overall risk management. After all, life happens to all of us.

Life happens to all of us.

Many situations are impossible to predict because they occur suddenly and when least expected. A serious illness could prevent you from going back to work, or a cancer diagnosis could prevent you from obtaining long-term care insurance. If your spouse is diagnosed with a debilitating disease, chances are you will need significant professional assistance, especially if he or she is physically fit and able to live with the condition for many years. These things have happened to people I know, and they have probably happened to people you know.

Many times those of us who have worked hard and created financial security for ourselves become responsible for other family members, whether by choice or by default. The baby boom generation is sometimes referred to as the "sandwich" generation because they are sandwiched between their parents, who are primarily Depression-era babies, and their adult children, some of whom still rely on them for support.

Some of us spend a good bit of our pre- and post-retirement days traveling back to our parents' homes to help them as they age, and some of us bring them home to live with us. In addition, many of us spend time helping our children solve any number of issues. The good news about having children is that they can provide us with grandchildren, which makes up for any bad they could ever do. (Of course, it could also mean another college fund to contribute to!)

MY RISK ASSESSMENT FORMULA

I admit, many of my ideas were born out of oversights or mistakes I made early in my career. The following story is one example.

In 1992, when I was a stockbroker, one of my clients (I'll call him "Joe") was getting ready to retire. Joe and his wife had great plans to go on cruises and travel the world. I knew they had four children, but it was not my practice at the time to learn much about my clients' personal lives except to exchange niceties. I was taught to invest the money and then move on to the next client. I did a good job for Joe; he and his wife retired and were on their way to living the retirement of their dreams.

Shortly after they retired, one of their sons-in-law died suddenly. He was forty-one years old and left Joe's daughter with three little girls, $800,000 in debt after having started a business, and no life insurance.

Of course, this became Joe's problem. His daughter and three grandchildren moved in with him, and Joe and his wife provided daycare so their daughter could work to support the children. Not only did the children lose their father; they lost their mother because she had to go back to work. And my client lost his dream retirement.

Of course, Joe never blamed me. But even though I had not been hired by Joe's daughter or son-in-law, I never forgave myself for not having anticipated this type of loss, especially with my personal background. It was that day in 1992 that I was inspired to create a new process to try to prevent this type of oversight from happening to a client again.

In my experience, people's lives are inextricably tied to the concerns of their children, and what happens in their extended families has an impact on them as well. I think it is incredibly important to identify the people or situations that could legally, morally, or financially have an impact on your ability to create and maintain your Preferred Lifestyle. When it comes to risk management, our formula looks like this:

Risk management begins with risk assessment, which has two components. First, you must *identify* potential risks in your life, and second, you must *quantify* those risks. Once you identify and quantify potential problems, or train wrecks, there are really only two ways of managing those risks. The first way, which tends to be the default, is to *assume* the risk and hope the negative event doesn't happen to you. The second, far more proactive response is to *transfer* that risk by some legal means. For obvious reasons, I'm an advocate of the second course of action.

THE TOP TWENTY-TWO RISKS LIST

The following list represents the twenty-two most common risks or concerns I see with my clients. This is by no means an exhaustive compilation, but these are some of the primary issues I encounter regularly. Each one of these can wreak havoc on a family's finances if it is not addressed and dealt with in a timely manner. Working with your team of financial advisors, you should be able to put a "completed" check mark next to each of the categories below.

1. *Health insurance*: Be sure you are covered and all family members are covered, and consider risks such as losing employer-sponsored coverage. You should also consider additional coverage to supplement your Medicare.

2. *Pension*: If you have a pension, be sure it is well funded if you are going to depend on it for all or a portion of your lifestyle needs. Ask anyone who has had to scale back their retirement dreams after pension benefits were slashed when their company filed for bankruptcy.

3. *Social Security benefits*: Deciding when to take Social Security will depend on each client's circumstances and life expectancy. If you have a family history of good health, it might make sense to wait to get the maximum benefit. If you have a family history of poor health or have a physical ailment, it might make sense to take your benefits early.

4. *High concentration of publicly traded stock*: This risk occurs most often with high-ranking executives who have large company holdings they have accumulated via stock options, but it can easily apply to other professionals as well. Many employees of Enron watched their retirement plans soar as the value of their Enron stock rose. Unfortunately, many also lost it all when the company filed for bankruptcy. Risk management strategies exist to protect against the risks of concentrated stock portfolios. Each risk management strategy is unique and sophisticated; be sure your advisor knows how to implement strategies and knows company rules about selling stock, especially if you are a corporate insider.

5. *Homeowner's insurance*: Make sure to have your policy evaluated by a third party to be sure there are no surprises. For example, the policy might say it is for full replacement coverage but only if you rebuild on the same slab.

6. *Umbrella liability insurance*: This is important for covering homes and automobiles. It is surprising to see how many new clients come to us without adequate liability coverage.

7. *College education expenses*: You may want to consider this not only for your children but also for grandchildren, nieces, nephews, etc. This will generally mean establishing a 529 plan, ESA, or other college tuition plan.

8. *Teenage drivers*: Teenagers can be a huge risk to their parents. Buy them their own insurance policy and title the car they drive in their own name (gift tax laws may apply). You might also set up a "no questions asked" taxi fund to avoid the risk of drunk driving.

9. *Early demise*: Life insurance is needed to offset the loss of the breadwinner's income. For those who have young children, it is an absolute necessity. To determine how much life insurance one should have, back into the calculation by asking yourself, "How much income am I trying to replace?" Many people purchase life insurance policies on their children and children's spouses. This assures that their grandchildren will have sufficient resources in case of an adult child's early demise.

10. *Long-term illness*: Long-term care insurance is important to explore for anyone over the age of fifty. For those who don't think they can afford it, imagine what the cost will be of *not* having it should you become disabled and actually need it. Failure to have a policy in place could destroy the nest egg of even moderately wealthy Americans.

11. *Rental real estate*: There is always the major risk of tenants or their guests getting hurt on your property and filing a lawsuit. You should consider owning all investment real estate in the name of an entity and outside of your own name (an attorney can help you set this up). An umbrella liability insurance policy is also an important tool to mitigate this risk (see #6).

12. *Owning "toys"*: "Toys," such as planes, boats, RVs, jet skis, and four-wheelers, create an enormous potential liability, particularly if you are wealthy or have a high profile. As in

the case of rental property, using an entity to hold the asset can be a good idea. Also, you need to have proper liability insurance in place.

13. *Closely held business*: The biggest risk here is illiquidity. You need a strategy for deriving income from the business. Also, you need a succession plan in place that sets forth terms in the case of death, disability, divorce, or retirement of partners or shareholders.

14. *Disability insurance*: Business owners are more at risk for this. Most employees have some form of disability insurance through their employer, but business owners rarely have any (or enough) disability insurance for themselves. This is a risk not only for the business owner but also for every employee of that business.

15. *Illiquid assets*: This is the risk associated with having a large percentage of net worth in illiquid assets not producing income. Think back to my example of the Renoir painting in chapter 2. You need to have a plan in place to derive income from these assets if necessary.

16. *Families affected by divorce*: Remarriage brings new challenges in planning. For example, a remarried man might want to provide for the income needs of his current spouse in the event of his death, but he might want the bulk of his assets to pass on to the children from his first marriage. Or a woman who receives an inheritance from her parents might want to pass it on to her children, not her current spouse. Without careful planning here, you could accidentally end up disinheriting your children or leaving your assets to someone you never intended to.

17. *"Yours, Mine, and Ours" family*: Imagine the complexity in a situation where each spouse had children prior to the marriage and the couple then has a child or children together. Estate planning could be challenging for this family.

18. *No wills or trusts*: An entire book could be written on the problems we have seen in estate planning. By not having a will, you die intestate, and the courts must decide who gets your money. In some states, it is not automatically assumed that the surviving parent is granted guardianship of the minor children. You should, at a minimum, have a will to communicate your wishes as to the guardianship for any minor children.

19. *Improper estate plans that are outdated*: This can cause some unintended consequences, such as the following:

    a. Assets being left "outright" or in some graduated format to the children after the second death: either of these formats leaves open the possibility of inheritances being attacked at some later date due to divorce, liability suits, bankruptcies, or creditor issues of the beneficiaries.

    b. Under ideal circumstances, amounts left to a spouse may be left with creditor protection, but that has to be built into the plan.

    c. Assets left to a spouse are sometimes unwittingly left to a future spouse, in which case the deceased person unintentionally disinherits his or her own children. Sadly, I have seen this happen before.

20. *Estate tax liability*: This can be a huge issue, especially for very wealthy individuals with many nonliquid assets. Upon the death of a couple or individual, the children or heirs

are left with a huge tax bill and not enough liquidity in the estate to pay it.

21. *Ancillary legal documents not updated*: Concerning health care directives, living wills, powers of attorney, etc., chances are the laws in your state may have changed recently and your documents may not be valid or could be challenged. We recommend that our clients update these at least annually.

22. *Estate plan not optimized*: In a situation where adequate estate planning has not been done, the lion's share of the estate could end up going to the Internal Revenue Service rather than to children, family, and/or charities.

I see these risks day in and day out. Most of them have solutions you can implement to mitigate or remove them. Of course, there are many risks we cannot anticipate—our personal Black Swans, if you will—nor can we do anything about them. We cannot anticipate terrorist attacks, wars, or many matters concerning our health. While we can eat well and exercise often, it doesn't always prevent health issues like cancer, heart disease, or Alzheimer's disease from invading our world.

The only thing we can do to prevent loss to our families as a result of health issues is to be mindful of having good health insurance and sufficient long-term care insurance so we don't exhaust the family resources. Too often I see a wife who exhausts all of the family finances trying to keep her husband alive. As an unwanted result, she faces the risk of running out of money before she herself runs out of time.

If you cannot adequately determine whether all of these risks have been addressed in your planning, I implore you to have a qualified financial advisor work with you and take you through a risk assessment of your own to see which, if any, of these risks may pertain to your situation.

WHAT ABOUT ME?

I often meet people who haven't quite arrived at the pre-retiree/retiree mark. The primary risk they're worried about is whether or not they'll be able to achieve their retirement goals in time. "I'm fifty years old," they tell me. "What if I have not yet accumulated the amount I need to reach financial independence? Where should I invest my hard-earned dollars?" Perhaps you, too, are asking the question, "What about me?"

Depending on when you read this book and what type of investment products are available at the time, I would suggest you go back to the section on Lifestyle investments and, based on the criteria presented there, determine what products exist that are best suited for your needs.

At the time of this writing, one suggestion I could make without knowing your particular circumstances would be to invest a portion of your money in products with guaranteed income riders. Why? Because you want the growth potential of the traditional financial markets, but you also want to have some sort of guarantee or some downside protection in case the markets collapse. Just remember, any guarantees are only as good as the claims-paying ability of the underlying entity. On the other hand, you don't want to be a year from retirement, have the markets go down by 30 or 40 percent, and have to continue working instead.

If you are around fifty years old
and thinking about your retirement
goals, you might consider investing
a portion of your money in products
with guaranteed income riders.
Just remember, any guarantees are
only as good as the claims-paying
ability of the underlying entity.

While you might be able to invest in traditional stocks, bonds, and exchange-traded funds to reach retirement unscathed, I believe the likelihood of a smooth ride will be slim. Do you really want to spend the remaining years of your working life worrying and wondering if you'll ever be able to retire? Why not transfer some of this risk to an insurance company who has the ability to use the law of large numbers and a lot of sophisticated hedging techniques to buffer your ride?

The other question I am commonly asked is in regard to people's 401(k) plans. Many people have a limited number of investment choices, and none of them have any underlying guarantees. First, I am hoping Congress or the financial industry as a whole will take the issue of retirement and market volatility to heart and design products that will offer some form of underlying guarantees to 401(k) participants. As of this writing, the hesitancy is that employers themselves do not want to be liable for providing those guarantees. I do believe legislation will evolve to provide guaranteed investment solutions, but for the most part, they don't currently exist in the majority of traditional 401(k) plans.

I have had many spirited discussions as to whether or not you should even participate in your 401(k), and I can see both sides of the argument. What I find uninspiring is the thought that I could invest the maximum amount allowable in a 401(k) and continue to invest my hard-earned dollars for upward of ten or fifteen years, only to have the markets collapse six months before I was ready to retire. Talk about a risk that can ruin your day—try your whole retirement!

Therefore, my suggestion would be to invest only an amount sufficient enough to be eligible for any matching dollars from your firm. Many times, if you invest 6 percent of your income, your firm will match up to 3 percent. The idea of investing any more than that and subjecting it to unprotected market risk is not appealing to me. I realize investing after-tax dollars outside of your 401(k) may not be all that appealing either, but you should weigh the pros and cons of both strategies to see what makes sense for you.

BRINGING IT ALL TOGETHER

I started this book with an intimate look at my own life and how I learned at an early age the importance of risk management. Though things happen for a reason and the hardships I faced growing up helped to make me who I am today, I hope the concepts laid out in this book will help you and your heirs avoid facing similar hardships. I have made it my life's goal to help people do exactly that.

Lifestyle Driven Investing is not just another reinterpretation of asset allocation. In fact, the "investing" aspect of Lifestyle Driven Investing, though obviously extremely important, is actually a secondary priority. First and foremost is the understanding of risk so that you can properly mitigate it. Lifestyle Driven Investing is about ensuring that you do not run out of money before you run out of time.

If you are serious about safeguarding your financial future, then consider this book as only the beginning. I've laid out a framework in which to consider your financial planning needs, but that is all this book is intended to be. I encourage you to do what I did. Find experts in the areas you want to know more about and learn from them; read and study as much as possible.

> ## "A good decision is based on knowledge and not on numbers."
> ## —Plato

There is no perfect investment product, and there is no magic number. As the Greek philosopher Plato said, "A good decision is based on knowledge and not on numbers." In the pages of *The Big Retirement Risk*, I have tried to arm you with knowledge so you can make the right decisions for yourself and the people you love. My hope is that you will continue to learn and educate yourself so you can eliminate the biggest risk of all: running out of money before you run out of time.

Best of luck to you on your journey!

ERIN'S ESSENTIALS

- Risk management is an important yet often undervalued aspect of financial planning. Taking the time to think about and prepare for what could happen now is much better than waiting for something to happen and having to deal with it later.
- Once you have identified and quantified the risks that pertain to you, you can begin the process of managing them through assuming the risk or transferring the risk.
- **Ask yourself:**
  - What good is financial planning if a single event could occur that could take away everything I have worked and planned for?
  - Is a comprehensive risk assessment a component of my financial plan?

Go to **www.thebigretirementrisk.com**
to download a complimentary risk assessment tool.

IMPORTANT DISCLOSURE
INFORMATION

Erin T. Botsford is the founder of The Botsford Group, a financial services firm located in Atlanta, Georgia, and Frisco, Texas. Certain portions of the book may reflect positions and/or recommendations as of a specific prior date, and may no longer be reflective of current positions and/or recommendations for various reasons, including regulatory changes. No reader should assume that the book serves as the receipt of, or a substitute for, personalized advice from Ms. Botsford or The Botsford Group, or from any other investment professional. Please remember that different types of investments involve varying degrees of risk. Therefore, it should not be assumed that future performance of any specific investment, investment product, or investment strategy (including the investments and/or investment strategies referenced in this book), or any of the book's non-investment related content, will be profitable, prove successful, or be applicable to any individual's specific situation. Should a reader have any questions regarding the applicability of any portion of the book content to his/her individual situation, the reader is encouraged to consult with the professional advisors of his/her choosing.

An actively managed portfolio cannot assure a profit or protect against loss. Inherent limitations and market conditions may affect the performance of a portfolio. There is no guarantee that an actively managed portfolio will produce greater returns or experience smaller losses than a portfolio that uses a buy-and-hold strategy. High turnover rates within a portfolio may increase transaction costs and taxable capital gains. Indexes are unmanaged, and investors are not able to invest directly into any index.

Investors should be aware that there are risks inherent in all investments, such as fluctuations in investment principal. With any investment vehicle, past performance is not a guarantee of future results.

Material discussed herein is meant for general illustration and/or informational purposes only. Please note that individual situations can vary. Therefore, the information should be relied upon only when coordinated with individual professional advice.

The S&P 500 is an unmanaged index comprised of five hundred widely held securities considered to be representative of the stock market in general.

Sector investing may involve a greater degree of risk than investments with broader diversification.

Investing in securities involves risk, including the loss of principal invested. Past performance is no guarantee of future results.

Investments in real estate have various risks, including the possible lack of liquidity and devaluation based on adverse economic and regulatory changes. As a result, the values of real estate may fluctuate, resulting in the value at sale being more or less than the original price paid.

Global or international investing involves special risks, such as currency fluctuation, political instability, and different methods of accounting and different reporting requirements.

The price of commodities, such as gold, is subject to substantial price fluctuations over short periods of time and may be affected by unpredictable international monetary and political policies. The market for commodities is subject to varying regulatory regimes, and concentrated investing may lead to higher price volatility. In addition, investing in commodities often involves international investing in emerging markets, which involve significant risks.

ACKNOWLEDGMENTS

My goal in writing this book was to convey new wisdom from decades of personal and professional experiences. I wanted to help people who are retired or are nearing retirement wade through the minefields of a financial system that makes it difficult to reach or sustain their dreams. The old models are broken; a new mind-set needs to emerge. I saw that our model, continually developed over more than twenty years, worked incredibly well through the 2008 financial crisis. I only wish more people had known about it and could have used it to help protect their lifestyles.

To that end, I want to give credit first to my incredible team at The Botsford Group, who believe in our philosophy about money and help me deliver our messages daily to our client base. I want to name them individually so they know how much I value their loyal service to me and to our clients: Kay Lynn Mayhue, Kyle Shores, Brad Cast, Jennifer Cox, Vicki Perrin, JP Pattinson, Nicole Denson, Ben Curtis, Blaine Malcolm, Susan Meghdadpour, Kim White, Sanders McCown, and Jena Blue. I also want to include a few former employees—Robin Skillingberg, Wes Pingelton, Carrie Wilson, and Rozanne Holmes—who will always be a part of our team in spirit.

I want to thank Charles Sizemore and Bryan Strike who assisted me with the initial steps of technical writing and editing.

Thank you for your willingness to help with this project. You were just the guys I needed! To my sister, Shannon Markle, who dove in feet first helping me to stay organized and finding amazing resources to turn my dream into a reality.

To my Botsford reading team, Kay Lynn Mayhue, Jennifer Cox, Kyle Shores, Vicki Perrin, Shannon Markle, and Ben Curtis, thank you for your countless hours of reading the initial drafts and giving me honest feedback. To my primary editors, Vicki Perrin and Ben Curtis, I could not have done this without you. Thank you for your unwavering dedication and for believing in me and in this project.

To my wonderful writing coach, Ann McIndoo, thank you for wrapping your arms around me and giving me the courage and confidence to write this book myself. You came along at just the right time and I will be forever grateful for your guidance, wisdom, and newfound friendship. You are simply a gem.

To Dan Sullivan, my business coach of many years: I am certain you have no idea what a profound impact you have made on my personal and my professional life, nor on the lives of those around me. Through your Strategic Coach program, my life and my business have been enriched in such incredible ways. Thank you for encouraging me to "always make my future bigger than my past."

To Ray Sclafani, Bryan Reece, and Joby Gruber, thanks guys for being great friends, mentors, and coaches. I will never be able to repay you for the guidance, wisdom, and advice you have given me over the years.

To my attorneys, Tom Giachetti and Paul Myers, who always give me confidence, and to Norman Sue from the DeWaay team, thank you for always being there for me and for watching my back.

To my friend, Kathy Peel, thank you for encouraging me from the beginning, going with me to New York, and believing I had a message to deliver. Your friendship and honest feedback have been so important to me.

To Harry Dent, Rodney Johnson, Nouriel Roubini, Robert Kiyosaki, Dr. David Babbel, Nassim Taleb, and Moshe Milevsky, thanks to the work all of you have done, I was able to view the future economic landscape and understand the impact demographics, debt, and the other brewing storm clouds could play in our financial markets. My eyes were opened by each of you and the folly of traditional planning going forward was exposed. I am a better planner because of each of you.

To the members of Greenleaf Book Group, thank you for taking a project that was war-torn and bringing it back to life. We had been down a long, dusty road when we finally found you. You have been everything we had hoped to find from the beginning.

To my friends and family who have stood by me and encouraged me from the sidelines, thank you for believing in me and for being the best cheerleaders I could ever have had.

To my many clients who have believed in our message, taken our advice, referred friends, and encouraged me to write this book, thank you for becoming part of our "family" and for spreading our gospel of Lifestyle Driven Investing.

To my only son, Kevin Botsford, over whom I believe the sun rises and sets! Thank you, Kev, for always believing in me, for encouraging me, and for putting up with a mom who was pretty darned driven to save the world, one client at a time. I am so proud of the man you have become and your willingness to serve our country in faraway places like Iraq and Afghanistan. To my daughter-in-law, Kristin, thank you for your constant support in getting me through this project. Thank you especially for praying for me, which meant so much along the way.

To my beloved husband, Bob Botsford, my best friend and my biggest fan. Thank you, honey, for being the wind beneath my wings and for often taking backseat to the demands of running a large business. You have been there through thick and thin with me, all the way back to the days of my youth, supporting me every step of the way. Thanks for always being my sounding board and my gut check, and thank you for continuing to remind me it is in giving that I receive.

I would never want to forget to thank God the father, His son, Jesus Christ, and His Holy Spirit, whom I will credit for giving me guidance, wisdom, strength to endure hardships, and eternal hope. In the spirit of one of my favorite verses, Ephesians 3:20, "Now to Him who is able to do immeasurably more than all we ask for or could imagine, to Him be the Glory forever and ever, Amen." Thanks, God . . . for everything.

INDEX